HIGH TECH
TENNIS

Second Edition

D0964358

Jack L. Groppel, PhD
Executive Vice President
of the Loehr-Groppel/Saddlebrook
Sport Science Center

Leisure Press
Champaign, Illinois

Library of Congress Cataloging-in-Publication Data

Groppel, Jack L.
   High tech tennis / Jack L. Groppel. -- 2nd ed.
      p.   cm.
   Rev. ed. of: Tennis for advanced players and those who would like
to be. c1984.
   Includes bibliographical references (p.   ) and index.
   ISBN 0-88011-458-4
   1. Tennis.   I. Title.
GV995.G76   1992
796.342'2--dc20   92-2861
                                                                      CIP

ISBN: 0-88011-458-4

This book is a revised edition of *Tennis for Advanced Players and Those Who Would Like to Be*,
published in 1984 by *Human Kinetics Publishers, Inc.*

Cover photo of Jonathon Stark was provided courtesy of United States Tennis Association.

Acquisitions Editor: Brian Holding
Developmental Editors: Lori Garrett
   and Holly Gilly
Assistant Editor: Elizabeth Bridgett
Copyeditor: Julie Anderson
Proofreader: Karin Leszczynski
Indexer: Sheila Ary

Production Director: Ernie Noa
Typesetter: Sandra Meier
Text Design: Keith Blomberg
Text Layout: Tara Welsch
   and Kimberlie E. Henris
Cover Design: Jack Davis
Printer: United Graphics

Leisure Press books are available at special discounts for bulk purchase for sales promotions,
premiums, fund-raising, or educational use. Special editions or book excerpts can also be
created to specification. For details, contact the Special Sales Manager at Leisure Press.

Printed in the United States of America

10   9   8   7   6   5   4   3   2

Leisure Press
A Division of Human Kinetics Publishers, Inc.
Box 5076, Champaign, IL 61825-5076
1-800-747-4457

Canada Office:
Human Kinetics Publishers, Inc.
P.O. Box 2503, Windsor, ON N8Y 4S2
1-800-465-7301 (in Canada only)

Europe Office:
Human Kinetics Publishers (Europe) Ltd.
P.O. Box IW14
Leeds LS16 6TR
England
0532-781708

Australia Office:
Human Kinetics Publishers
P.O. Box 80
Kingswood 5062
South Australia
374-0433

Contents

This book is dedicated to my parents,
Howard and Pauline Groppel,
for their undying devotion and support.

Foreword

In the 1970s, tennis was a sport begging for scientific help. Myths about the game and how to play it were being produced faster than monthly journals could publish them. Only a handful of people were even concerned about the scientific principles that governed the many aspects of the sport.

Along came the 1980s, and the public began to take a look inside the laboratory to see what those crazy tennis scientists were up to. What they were doing was trying to find ways to help players, from amateur to elite, maximize performance and their enjoyment of the sport in the shortest possible time.

Things got more fun as people discovered that the information being disseminated by the scientists actually worked. A few professional players even dared to mention it in the media. Now the sport sciences have exploded, and good information keeps coming.

Dr. Jack Groppel, a sport scientist and former tournament player, became an international leader during this information explosion and continues in that position today. His thirst for knowledge and his continued curiosity are certainly demonstrated in this second edition. Reading this book is fun and exciting—and it will help you beat that opponent you've had your eye on. Whether or not you win your every match, you'll be a heck of a lot smarter about the game of tennis.

—Vic Braden

Preface

The Germans and the Czechs have traditionally been known for their scientific approach to player development, but it wasn't until the mid- to late 1980s that tennis organizations worldwide began accepting the role of sport science in developing players. The International Tennis Federation conducted regional workshops in Asia, Africa, Europe, and South America covering biomechanics, fitness, nutrition, and psychology. The United States Tennis Association formed a sport science committee to investigate various issues in sport biomechanics, sport physiology, sport nutrition, sport psychology, sports medicine, and motor learning. This sport science approach has now been identified as the foundation of improving tennis skills.

Athletes often shy away from attempts to mix science with sport. However, *High Tech Tennis* is not a physics book of tennis. Rather, it provides specific, easy-to-use guidance for improving your game through applying sport science to your strokes and movement. You will benefit from several special features: discussions of the basics of stroke mechanics and footwork; extensive illustration, including stop-action sequences of good players demonstrating proper technique; and "Dr. Jack's Tips," useful performance cues I have used successfully with players throughout the years. I offer you a simple approach to understanding the scientific fundamentals of tennis.

Which professional player has the best form? Is it Becker, Graf, Agassi, Capriati . . . ? There is no perfect way to play tennis! All of these pros swing the racket with specific idiosyncrasies. Depending on the grip used, a racket can be swung in numerous ways and still hit the ball effectively. That's why you shouldn't try to mimic someone's technique—you don't know if there are reasons why she or he performs that way. John McEnroe's service stance has frequently been ridiculed, but many players have idolized John and tried to play like him. Yet they never realized that he began using that stance as a youth for therapeutic reasons (because of a strained back), not to improve his serve! You must base your playing technique on what works for *you*. This book will guide you in that pursuit.

Perfection is needed at only one instant during the swing: when the ball is on the racket face. The ball must be hit correctly. Bjorn Borg's forehand was once considered too unorthodox for him ever to make it big and likely to lead to career-ending tennis elbow. But with five consecutive Wimbledon titles and six French Open titles to his credit, Borg proved to be nearly perfect in hitting the ball how and where he wanted. What separates great players from good ones is that good players don't hit the ball as effectively as they could if they knew more efficient stroke techniques. Applying sport science concepts can greatly improve strokes. I may not be able to convert yours into world-class forehands and backhands, but I can help you develop much more efficient and effective tools for competition.

In the first few chapters of this second edition, you will learn basic sport science concepts and how they apply to tennis. You will discover the importance of equipment design. How do string tension and racket flexibility affect your game? What should you look for when selecting shoes? What impact does the court surface have on your game? I have greatly expanded and developed the chapter on movement and footwork because I believe that movement is the major limiting factor of most tennis players. I have included 11 drills designed to help you improve your movement.

Subsequent chapters deal with advanced stroke development, including how to get more power while maintaining control and how to effectively use spin. You will learn to view your body as a linked system through which power and momentum are transferred to your stroke and can be increased. In chapter 10, new to this edition, you will learn some important and perhaps surprising facts about the game as well as discover some common fallacies. In the final chapter I help you put all of your new knowledge into perspective, and I discuss the often overlooked mental game of tennis.

High Tech Tennis is not a tennis "cookbook," because I do not feel such an approach works. Tennis is a game requiring practice and the will to improve. My purpose is to give you proven, researched information to improve your game. The laws of science govern human motion, whether you are walking, shooting a basket, or hitting a tennis ball. These laws have been applied with remarkable success by Olympic athletes intent on breaking world records, and there is no reason you can't easily apply them to your own game.

An incredible amount of sport science data can be used by the tennis player. Bridging the gap between the sport scientist and the athlete has been a problem, but I feel the dilemma is being resolved in tennis because the game is loaded with players with a passion to improve, and to improve in the most efficient way. The modern tennis player has specific needs that are met in this book. My approach is to deal with those needs in an applied manner that all tennis players and students of the game will understand, appreciate, and enjoy. No professional player has perfect form in all situations. With *High Tech Tennis*, I will help you develop your own style to maximize your ability and perform at your best.

Acknowledgments

$\mathbf{M}$any people have had major roles in the development of my career, and to all of them I owe a great deal of gratitude. But mere thanks isn't enough for those who have had a significant impact on teaching me to apply sport science to the game of tennis. In addition, I want to give credit to those who have helped me understand the business of tennis and to those who actually helped put this book together.

Special thanks should go to the individuals who were heavily involved in my education: Chuck Dillman, Bob Singer, Terry Ward, and especially my current mentor, Tom Dempsey, from whom I seem to learn something every minute we are together.

I would also like to extend my gratitude to those whose lives are already dedicated to tennis and with whom I have worked along the way: Vic Braden, Tim and Tom Gullikson, Tim Heckler, Jim Loehr, Robert Nirschl, Paul Roetert, Stan Smith, Ron Woods, and especially my colleagues at Harry Hopman/Saddlebrook International Tennis—Alvaro Betancur, Maureen Dempsey, Dwaine and Trish Gullett, Howard Moore, Tommy Thompson, and all the outstanding coaches in the organization.

A special acknowledgment should go to the following persons: Mike Nishihara, whose knowledge and assistance have been invaluable in the development of the movement drills in chapter 3; Peter Bouton, Denton Desquitado, Oriane Eriksen, Jack Conrad, and Sue Arildsen, who served as models for some of the photos; Dick Boehning, for his leadership in matters regarding the business aspects of tennis; Jill Workman, executive director of the U.S. Racket Stringers Association, who provided me with a plethora of information on rackets and strings; Chuck Mercer, Gary Maynard, and Jim Aquino, for their excellent photography; and Chris Dann and Cindy Hook, who helped a great deal in the typing of this manuscript.

Finally, I want to offer my sincere appreciation to those who have given me understanding and encouragement even during the roughest of times in developing this second edition: Jan Blum, Bill Wicks, Ruth Ann Kincaid, and my parents.

C H A P T E R 1

The Quest
for the Perfect Game

To win the Wimbledon singles championship is the ultimate experience for a tennis player. But the preparation required to compete well at Wimbledon and to win is phenomenal. Have you ever considered what goes into training for a Wimbledon crown? First, you have to hit the ball effectively, Second, you must be in peak physical condition. Third, you must move with the grace and speed of a cheetah, and finally, you must have the mind of a warrior. These are the four limiting factors of tennis: stroke production, physical fitness, on-court movement, and mental fitness. I believe that all players, regardless of skill level, should have monthly checkups on these four parameters, continually evaluating (with the help of their teaching professionals) the weaknesses in each area and how to go about improving each area. This forms an objective, almost scientific, foundation on which a tennis player can assess his or her improvement. Combine this with the tennis teaching professional's vast knowledge of sport science information from biomechanics, physiology, nutrition, sports medicine, motor learning, and sport psychology, and today's tennis player can improve at a rapid rate.

1

How Sport Science Affects Tennis

Sport research, in general, has increased dramatically over the past few years. Its acceptance by athletes in all sports is universal. The Germans are renowned for their swimming research and the Soviets for their application of research to track and field. Unfortunately, tennis has only recently begun reaping the benefits of research, but there is definitely an increasing involvement between coaches, scientists, and engineers in the study of our game. Recent research has made a tremendous contribution to improving a player's conditioning program, developing mental strategies, designing better equipment, and understanding performance techniques. The key to this research, however, is getting the information to the player.

Many books exist that discuss physical conditioning and mental fitness, but few authors have dealt with the sport science principles behind stroke production and movement on the court. Stroke mechanics and footwork are the foundation of your success in tennis. For example, your strokes don't have to be aesthetically pleasing, but they must be effective. And the more efficient your strokes are the less energy you will expend while competing. When your tennis strokes are both effective and efficient, the results can be devastating to your opponent. However, it's another matter when your game lacks one of these elements. If your shots lack effectiveness, your game won't be strong enough to hurt your opponent; even worse, if they lack efficiency, you may be injured. This is where sport science can help your game; it can make you both efficient and effective. For example, take the case of Stan Smith, the world's Number 1 ranked player from 1971 to 1973.

Efficiency

When describing Stan Smith's service motion, the words *classic* and *picture perfect* come to mind. His serve was so extremely effective that it enabled him to dominate the game in the early 1970s. By the late 1970s, his domination diminished, partly due to severe elbow pain. The pain became so severe that Smith needed surgery.

Prior to the operation, Smith decided to find out what had caused his problem: whether simply stress from overuse or whether a flaw in stroke production. To determine the cause, I took high-speed films of Smith during a workout. The films, played back at normal speed, revealed no apparent error in stroke mechanics. But, when the films were viewed in stop-action, a problem with his serve became clear. When Smith reached a point in his service motion near the top of his backswing, his hand turned under excessively (Figure 1.1). This extraneous movement placed

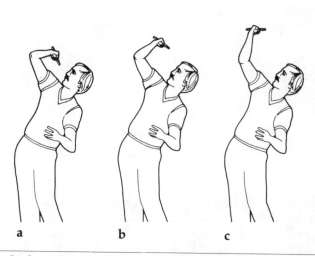

Figure 1.1 In these diagrams (drawn from consecutive movie frames taken at 100 frames per second), you can see the problem Stan Smith had with the positioning of his racket, hand, wrist, and elbow.

an incredible amount of force on the inner part of his elbow. Scar tissue built up as his body's defense mechanisms tried to protect the joint. Unfortunately, this protective scarring put so much pressure on the nerves in Smith's elbow that the elbow had to be surgically repaired.

Following the surgery, Smith wanted to change his serve to prevent any recurrence of elbow trauma. Although no change could offer 100 percent assurance, a backswing technique was recommended to lower the stresses to the elbow. Instead of the full windmill action that allowed his hand to turn under at the top of the stroke, Smith began using a half-swing method to take the racket back (Figure 1.2). This new motion still allowed him an adequate amount of body rotation yet prevented too much hand movement at the top of his backswing. In addition, Smith was advised that when he got to the top of his swing he should keep the palm of his hand toward his head, further preventing his hand from turning under. Smith practiced this new backswing until the action at the top of the backswing became natural. He tried it immediately upon his return to the circuit and subsequently won the Australian Tournament of Champions. Interestingly enough, it was not the windmill-type backswing that caused the problem but Smith's excessive hand action at

a   b

c   d

Figure 1.2   Stan Smith changed his full windmill-type serving action to the half-swing method seen in these pictures.

the top of the stroke. Once he controlled the hand action, he was able to successfully return to the former backswing technique.

Smith was one of the world's best tennis players whose serve was considered to be the perfect form. The one small flaw in Stan Smith's serve, and the one that caused him so much pain, was never picked up by the naked eye. Instead, it took a specific view from a high-speed film analysis to identify the problem.

Effectiveness

Stan Smith's problem was one of stroke efficiency, but sport science can do more than simply help players become more efficient: It can help them become more effective. For example, I have worked with many highly ranked players in Florida but one in particular comes to mind. This athlete had a great weapon in his forehand, but he used his two-handed backhand only when necessary to keep the ball in play. His backhand wasn't a very penetrating shot, so he asked me to take a look at his stroke and recommend a change that would develop him into a stronger player on his backhand side. His problem became apparent after I watched about 10 minutes of rallying. His body rotation was very limited when he used his two-handed backhand, so much that it seemed he didn't use his hips and trunk but employed excessive arm action (Figure 1.3). By separating the movements of his trunk and upper limbs during the forward swing, he had very little force behind the stroke. I told him to step forward into the shot as he had been doing but to let his trunk and arms work together as one unit rather than swinging so much like a baseball player. Being a skilled tennis player, he took only about 15 minutes to realize how the hips and trunk should work together in bringing the arms and racket toward impact (Figure 1.4). He was amazed

a   b   c

Figure 1.3 This is an ineffective two-handed backhand. Note how little hip rotation occurs, which makes the trunk and upper limbs work harder.

a   b   c

Figure 1.4   This is an efficient two-handed backhand that sufficiently employs the hips and trunk to transfer force to the upper limbs.

at how much harder he was able to hit the ball after only another few minutes of practice. All he needed was a mechanical analysis (which any certified teaching professional can do) to bring together his body parts in hitting an effective two-handed backhand. Thus, his effectiveness was increased by improving his technique.

Understanding Equipment Design

Sport science can also help tennis players improve playing abilities by helping them understand how equipment is designed and properly used. For example, in the mid-1970s, Howard Head invented the over-sized racket and presented it to the tennis world. Head, who turned the entire skiing industry around with the production of metal skis, had the audacity to suggest that tennis players might be able to hit the ball more effectively with a bigger racket. Head's oversized racket, popularized by Prince Manufacturing and later developed by all companies, was the brunt of many jokes. The ridicule, however, didn't last very long; players soon realized that Head was right! His racket was found to have a larger hitting zone and to decrease vibrations and oscillations transmitted to the hand from impact. The big racket also gave some players a psychological edge as well; beginners and advanced players began to feel secure when using the larger head because they felt they simply couldn't miss!

How You Can Use Sport Science Principles to Help Your Game

Although we've seen how specific applications of sport science have helped some athletes, the next step becomes applying this knowledge to you. One question you need to ask yourself is, What must I do to make my strokes more effective and efficient? To help you become a better player you must understand what is meant by *efficiency* and *effectiveness* for a tennis player and then apply some very basic physical laws to your strokes and your movement.

Identifying Proper Form

Efficiency and effectiveness in tennis involve proper form. Good form is not a set pattern of movement but rather movement that accomplishes the purpose with the least expenditure of energy. You must learn to play properly to conserve energy for those long matches and to expend energy with the greatest efficiency.

Identifying proper form can be difficult, however, because good form is unique to individuals and does not necessarily follow any norms. For example, the one crucial point of any tennis stroke is impact. You must get to the impact point efficiently and effectively, through good form. Your form must be "good" not necessarily from the standpoint of aesthetics but in terms of developing optimal force and control within your own capabilities.

Developing Force by Understanding Laws of Motion

Developing force in tennis is not as hard as some players think. The laws of motion developed by Sir Isaac Newton to describe what happens in the universe are the same laws that govern how well you play tennis; they explain how control and force are gained by a tennis player.

Law of Inertia

The law of inertia states that a body will stay at rest or in motion until acted upon by an outside force. When you are in the ready position, for example, your body and racket are not moving and have a certain amount of resting inertia. When you react to your opponent's shot, you must overcome that resting inertia by using gravity and by creating sufficient force against the ground to move. Muscular contraction from the legs causes that motion to occur.

During a point, a player has moving inertia and will keep going until some force stops the movement. Think of an athlete in full sprint running to hit a wide forehand. Once the ball is hit, the player must get to a strategic part of the court in anticipation of the return. A recovery step often stops the player from moving in one direction and reverses him or her in the opposite direction. After the ball is hit, the trail leg swings around, applies the brakes to stop the moving inertia, then generates force so the player can return to an advantageous court position.

Law of Acceleration

The law of acceleration states that force equals mass times acceleration. Obviously, you have no control over your mass during competition, so it is always a constant. Therefore, the force you develop is directly proportional to your acceleration, whether referring to your on-court speed or your racket head speed. The faster the racket head is traveling at impact, the greater the force applied to the ball.

Sounds simple enough, but a tennis player must bear one very important thing in mind. There is usually a speed–accuracy trade-off involved in most tennis strokes; the harder you swing (unless you are an accomplished tournament player), the less control you have. And obviously, it really doesn't matter how hard you hit the ball if it doesn't stay in the court! Tennis is unlike baseball, in which a home run can be hit over any part of the fence between the foul poles. Tennis is first and foremost a control game. A service ace must be hit with high velocity but must also be accurately placed. A high-speed serve can be returned relatively easily if it is not well placed. Hitting the ball hard is easy, but hitting it hard and with accuracy is difficult. Therefore, the law of acceleration should be applied within the context of shot control.

Law of Action and Reaction

Probably the most important of Newton's laws of motion in tennis is the law of action and reaction, which holds that for every action there is an equal and opposite reaction. This law provides the foundation for almost every tennis stroke, because a ground reaction force is required to overcome inertia and initiate movement. When the player is in the ready position and pushes against the ground to move, the ground pushes back with an equal and opposite force. Likewise, in a ground stroke, when the hind foot pushes to initiate the forward weight transfer, the ground reaction force initiates the body's total generation of force to hit the stroke. The ground reaction force also influences shot control because its direction of application against the ground determines the direction of body movement.

Let's examine how the law of action and reaction affects the serve (Figure 1.5). Once the forceful extension of the legs meets the ground reaction force, the force is transferred up through the body. The hips and trunk begin rotating with extreme speed, and that speed is subsequently transferred to the arm. Just as the swinging arm initiates its forward action toward impact, the opposite arm comes across the trunk in the opposite direction of the trunk's rotation. The opposing arm's action

a   b

c   d

Figure 1.5   This is a sequence of Boris Becker's serve. Notice how the knees flex and the torso rotates to prepare the body for the explosion seen in (c) and (d).

serves as a braking mechanism (because it's moving in the opposite direction) and abruptly slows the trunk rotation, causing the swinging arm and racket to accelerate toward impact. In this case the opposite arm's movement is the action, and the swinging arm reacts by accelerating and transferring the body's total momentum generated during the serving action to the racket.

Linear and angular momentum are two properties of objects in motion that will enable you to hit the ball better. Linear momentum simply involves transferring your body weight into the shot. As you learned tennis basics, your teacher probably told you to step into the ball on every shot (Figure 1.6). Your coach was telling you to increase the linear momentum of the stroke. Once you've transferred your linear momentum forward, angular momentum comes into play in the form of body rotation. When hitting a ground stroke, you will generate more linear momentum with the step forward and angular momentum with hip and trunk rotation. There are very few tennis strokes with which the athlete can be effective without using body rotation. To realize its importance, try hitting a forehand drive without rotating your trunk. Just don't do it in front of your teaching pro—he or she won't be happy!

Figure 1.6   Jennifer Capriati demonstrates how to use forward momentum in driving a two-handed backhand.

Dr. Jack's Tennis Tips

Always try to move forward into every shot to maximize the forward linear momentum. This will make the game a lot easier.

Obviously, the mechanics of tennis involve more than Newton's laws of motion. However, this preliminary information will serve as a foundation for the subsequent chapters dealing with equipment, movement, and stroke production. By having a thorough understanding of these physical laws, applying them to your strokes, and analyzing the strokes of highly skilled tennis players, you should improve your game dramatically.

What You Can Learn From Watching a Pro

Before we discuss how you can benefit from critiquing a professional tennis player's game, you must understand two things: there is no perfect way to swing the racket, and there's a difference between an important performance characteristic of a player and a mere idiosyncrasy.

There Is No Perfect Swing

Over a century ago, a wealthy golfer, Sir Ainsley Bridgland, developed one of the first research teams in all of sport, consisting of anatomists, engineers, and physiologists. Their goal was to discover the hidden secrets of the perfect golf swing. After all, a golfer merely had to address a stationary ball set up on a tee, so it seemed that there would be only one absolutely perfect way to swing the club. But after much research, the team concluded that there was no perfect way to swing the club; a variety of swing techniques could achieve the optimal outcome. The same is true for tennis, especially when you consider that the ball is seldom hit in the same place stroke after stroke. And look at the great players. Becker consistently strikes the ball hard, but uses spin well; Agassi effectively uses a two-handed backhand; and Capriati is an outstanding all-court player who can mix the speed and spin of her ground strokes with ease. All three athletes are great tennis players but they all play differently.

Emulate Important Characteristics, Not Idiosyncrasies

A performance characteristic is the basic skill a player uses to perform. Leg action, hip rotation, trunk rotation, and arm acceleration are a few typical performance characteristics. An idiosyncrasy is a unique aspect of a player's movement that really does not contribute to the stroke. We can look at a couple of the more well-known idiosyncrasies in tennis, which, in my opinion, will continue long after both these players have retired from the game. Chris Evert, for example, had a great following during her tenure in professional tennis. Many players, especially the young ones, wanted to be just like her, so they tried to mimic her strokes. She would be a great model to copy if the right things were modeled, but they usually weren't. For example, when Evert hit her forehand, she held her left arm out to the side and positioned her hand so it was opened and almost perpendicular to her forearm (Figure 1.7). This idiosyncrasy really had little to do with Evert's great forehand. Instead of copying her left hand's position, players should have noticed how the left arm moved relative to the right arm (Figure 1.7b), which showed how she used her trunk rotation to accelerate the racket head toward the ball.

a
b

Figure 1.7 Observe these photos of Chris Evert's left-hand position as she hits a forehand drive. Note in (b) how her left arm moves in synchrony with the right arm, which demonstrates the amount of trunk rotation she is using.

John McEnroe is another excellent example of a player who has been idolized but whose strokes have been improperly modeled. Many tennis authorities have always believed that McEnroe's stroke mechanics were poor, and if not for his outstanding athletic ability, he would have never succeeded in professional tennis. One reason for this public opinion has been his awkward serving stance (Figure 1.8). It's true that few teaching professionals would ever recommend this starting position. However, close examination of McEnroe's serve reveals that he actually generates a lot of body rotation during the motion. Therefore, his starting position isn't as bad as it might seem. It's his mechanics of motion prior to impact that make him a great server, not his starting position.

When watching a highly skilled player, don't be too attentive to extraneous motions; concentrate on how the player actually moves to swing

a   b

Figure 1.8 John McEnroe's starting position for his serve is shown in (a). Although his service stance has been criticized, you will learn from subsequent chapters how he utilizes this starting position to maximize his body rotation.

the racket. Make note of various body movements and how the player generates force to hit the ball. Pick out certain body parts and watch only these areas during a specific stroke, attempting to determine how each segment contributes to the final outcome. This approach could literally open your eyes to many aspects of how to play the best tennis you possibly can.

Dr. Jack's Tennis Tips

When watching a pro compete, don't watch the ball! Keep your eyes on the player and observe how he or she moves and hits the ball. Make note of footwork, leg action, hip rotation, and shoulder rotation.

NET RESULTS

As you continue your quest to improve your game, strive for a good speed–accuracy trade-off. This would increase your effectiveness and your competitive ability. In addition, remember that tennis is not played with the arm alone. You should generate force from the ground and transfer this force through your body to the swinging arm through a combination of linear and angular momentum. This sequencing of forces between body parts will not only enable you to hit more penetrating shots but will also improve your efficiency in playing the game.

C H A P T E R   2

Optimize Your Game
With the Proper Equipment

Renowned teaching professional Vic Braden has coined a phrase about tennis equipment that I find quite interesting. He says, "It doesn't matter what equipment you use; it's all engineered way beyond your physical capabilities." And you know what? He's right, if you consider how rackets, shoes, and tennis balls perform in laboratory experiments. But what about when you begin using the equipment on the court during a match? What about such things as how a racket feels when you hit an aggressive volley or how well your new shoes allow you to slide on clay? These factors and many more are important elements in selecting tennis equipment. Perhaps that's why F.W. Donisthorpe, in his 1933 essays on the *Mechanics of Lawn Tennis*, spent five pages describing stroke production and strategy while devoting nine pages to the design and function of balls and rackets. He continually cited the tennis player's dilemma in deciding what equipment to use.

The problems of selecting equipment for the tennis player in 1933 were nothing compared to those of today's player. The 1933 player had only one racket composition and shape available: wood in an elliptical form. Today, we have metal, fiberglass, graphite, boron, kevlar, ceramics, magnesium, and various other materials. In addition, rackets can have elliptical, tear-drop, or hexagonal shapes, or the infamous wide body design. Selecting a tennis shoe or type of ball in 1933 wasn't nearly as complicated, simply because there weren't as many to choose from.

Tennis equipment has proliferated for numerous reasons. First, engineering technology has advanced to enable manufacturers to discover, synthesize, and utilize new materials. Not only have the types of materials changed, but so have the designs. Tennis shoes, for example, used to be made only with rubber soles and only one style of shoe last. Rubber can still be found in some shoe soles, but several shoes have polyurethane composites in their sole designs. In addition, several shoe lasts are currently available that fit different types of feet and conform to different types of foot motion. There really seems to be no end in sight for the sophistication of tennis equipment. The only end may be caused by the pocketbooks of many tennis players who won't spend hundreds of dollars for a racket frame or a pair of shoes.

The tennis boom of the late 60s and early 70s is a second reason for so many types of tennis paraphernalia. With millions of players involved in the game at that time (and still involved to this day), the manufacturing business became very lucrative. Greater varieties of equipment were produced to meet the demands of the players and to maintain an edge over the competition. Many feel that with the recent surge of young players like Capriati and Sampras, the 90s will bring another miniboom to the game, which will again help to make the tennis industry manufacturers more creative and innovative.

Components of Racket Design

It's obvious that the tennis industry is still thriving. Although the major tennis boom is over, millions still play the game. Equipment will continue to improve, but even more important, consumers are more educated than in 1970. Manufacturers have identified the need to help the game at the grass-roots level by informing players about what to look for in equipment and how certain pieces of equipment might benefit them. We will discuss these factors to help you understand more about how equipment is designed and what some of the more recent research tells you about how to use the equipment to improve your game. In this section, we'll go over the differences between flexible and stiff rackets, how the racket head size might affect your game, and how the string type and tension you use can make you or break you.

Racket Materials and Flexibility

The trend of today's racket industry is toward the meteoric materials of viscoelastic polymers and graphite/fiberglass composites. Wood is outdated and will only work its way back into the spotlight as a composite with another material. Laminated wood strips used in the early racket simply do not provide a player with the power of today's modern designs.

Out of all the materials available, graphite is known to dampen the vibrations of impact more than any other. This is good news for the player afflicted with arm problems. Few rackets, however, are made solely of graphite; graphite is usually combined with fiberglass or some other high-performance material. This often forms a stiff racket that behaves extremely well on a short, aggressive stroke like the volley.

Manufacturers usually classify their rackets as stiff, medium flexibility, and flexible, although these classifications are not consistent among manufacturers. A racket categorized as stiff by one manufacturer might be placed in the medium-flexibility class by another. However, don't be concerned with these inconsistencies; what matters is how a certain racket feels in your hand when you are playing. That's why the tennis trade magazines hire expert panels to play-test new racket frames as they enter the market. In this way you receive the engineering information from the manufacturer and the playing information from the magazines; the rest is up to you in play-testing the racket yourself.

A racket classified near the stiff end of the continuum will yield a higher ball velocity than a more flexible racket. With a flexible racket, energy is lost as the shaft bends in reaction to impact. A stiff racket will not bend as much and the ball will not lose as much energy.

What causes one racket to be stiffer than another? Surprisingly enough, it's not the materials used to make the racket as much as it is the racket shape. The smoother the transition from the widest part of the racket head to the handle, the stiffer the racket will be. Materials used to make the racket do play a role, however. For example, the stiffness and weight properties of graphite are rated higher than aluminum. And graphite, once thought to be the epitome of stiffness, has lost its notoriety to the even stiffer attributes of boron. With varying composite construction, many more cross-sectional shapes are possible.

While most manufacturers were studying various innovations of materials and racket head shapes, some became creative and began looking at different ways to manipulate the thickness of the frame. The result of this engineering research was the wide body design (Figure 2.1). Frame stiffness was modified by increasing the cross section, and equally important, the stiffness could be locally controlled on the racket head (e.g.,

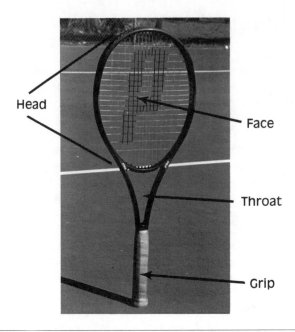

Figure 2.1   This picture shows a racket on the court. The area containing the strings is the face and is surrounded by the racket head. The throat is the area between the grip and racket head.

at the tip of the racket head or close to the throat). This type of stiffness control is found in most of today's rackets, but some manufacturers have gone one step further. One company has come out with a racket whose stiffness depends not only on its physical properties, but also on the dynamics of your stroke. If you swing hard, it has a stiff response, but if you hit a soft shot, it has more flexible properties.

When purchasing a racket be aware of its design and construction. If two rackets are made of similar composites and have similar shapes, there will usually be little difference in stiffness between the two. However, if a manufacturer has added a composite such as fiberglass or graphite to the frame, the stiffness of the racket will be affected dependent upon the reinforcement; fiberglass will tend to make a racket more flexible and graphite will make it stiffer. The more graphite found in a racket, the stiffer the racket will be. As for aluminum composites, however, stiffness depends more on racket shape than on materials. One piece of aluminum is as strong, within 2 percent, as another piece of aluminum. Some aluminum alloys are stronger than others, but they are not necessarily stiffer in relation to how they would react to impact by a tennis ball. The shape and cross section of the metal actually determine the racket's stiffness. As a rule, the bulkier the tubing or metal extrusion, the stiffer the racket.

Before you decide what racket flexibility you should have, analyze your own game style. If you like to rush and crush (serve and volley), a stiffer racket may be what you need. Remember that volleys are very short strokes and you need a quick response from the racket. However, if a baseline game better describes your playing style, you may want to try a more flexible racket. A quick racket response to develop ball velocity shouldn't be as high on your priority list as ball control.

Racket Head Design—The Shape of the Future

Now that you have an idea of what racket flexibility might best fit your game, you have to consider the size of the racket head with which you wish to play. Although you might already have an idea, I'll go over what sport science tells us about the various racket designs on the market.

Dr. Jack's Tennis Tips

Even though sport science provides a lot of information about racket playability, you should always play-test a racket to see if it really "feels good" for your game. Most tennis pro shops and specialty stores have rental programs where "your game" can test the racket.

The wood racket of the 1970s is a dinosaur. Whether it will experience a rebirth is up to future technology, but it seems doubtful that research on wood designs will yield the high performance found in graphite and other composites. Even the old Wilson Jack Kramer Autograph racket made of wood has gone by the wayside. Its contemporary counterparts have taken over the entire market.

When the first oversized racket hit the market in the mid-1970s, most people saw it as another fad. It was called a snowshoe, a screen door, a rug beater, and so on. But, what a mistake you made if you didn't buy stock in that part of the industry! Today, almost everyone plays with a racket head larger than the old elliptical head size seen on the wood racket. In fact, in the first edition of this book I said that within 10 years the conventional racket would be midsized or oversized and *not* the small elliptical frame of the previous decades. Well, I was wrong! It happened within 5 years, not 10.

What's so special about an oversized racket? Does it really enable you to play better? Or is it just a psychological placebo that has little effect on your playing?

There's no question that playing with an oversized racket has some psychological effects. Well-known television commentator Mary Carillo once remarked during one of Pam Shriver's matches, "Shriver is tall but she's even taller with that oversized racket!" Obviously, Pam wasn't any taller, but with the larger Prince racket in her hand she became an ominous figure at the net. Thus, it is possible you can intimidate your opponent by using one of these rackets. Figure 2.2 shows a variety of oversized rackets. Another psychological effect is that some players get increased confidence from using the bigger rackets. They go through what I call the "I-can't-miss syndrome."

Psychological reasons aside, there are some valid mechanical reasons for selecting a racket with a larger racket head. Some of the more recent studies in this field should interest you.

The Application of Sport Science to Racket Head Design

The majority of racket research has involved the difference in the increased racket head size of the midsized and oversized rackets compared to the old smaller head design. Regardless of racket head size, two things

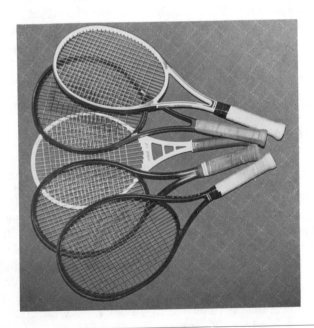

Figure 2.2   Rackets come in many different sizes and shapes.

hold true. When the ball hits in the center of percussion (usually located somewhere just below the geometric center of the racket face), the net force to the hand following impact is negligible. However, when a ball hits off-center on the racket face (which most do regardless of racket head size), the racket tends to twist along its long axis. This twisting effect, or torque, could have severe effects on the outcome of your shot and could cause serious strain to your forearm muscles as they contract to control the excessive racket movement.

Howard Brody, a physicist at the University of Pennsylvania, suggested that this twisting may be reduced by increasing the moment of inertia of the racket head. The moment of inertia (I) of an object is a measure of that object's resistance to rotation (Figure 2.3). Its magnitude is determined by a simple equation, $I = mr^2$, where m is the object's mass and r is its radius. Therefore, two ways exist to increase the moment of inertia of a racket head so the twisting effect will be reduced: increase the size of the racket head (thus increasing its radius), or add small weights to the perimeter of the racket head (thus increasing its mass). Both methods have been used, but the most popular is to increase the racket head size. Howard Head, the inventor of the oversized racket, found that making a racket 20 percent wider reduced the twisting potential by almost 40 percent. As for the sports medicine implications of this phenomenon, Dr. Robert Nirschl, one of the country's top orthopedists,

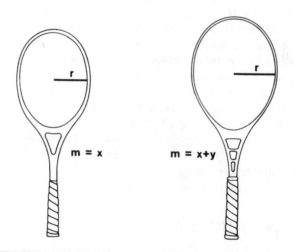

Figure 2.3   This diagram shows how the moment of inertia of a racket head can be increased to reduce rotation during and following impact. The larger the mass (m) or the radius (r), the greater the resistance to rotation. Here X is the mass of a conventional racket while X+Y is the mass of a larger racket.

has collected extensive data on afflicted patients when using midsized and oversized rackets. His data actually favor the midsized racket head as providing more protection to the player. The implication of Dr. Nirschl's conclusion is that the incidence of off-center impacts caused the rackets to rotate even more because of the large radius.

Besides reducing the twisting effect, widening the racket head or adding perimeter weights has another effect on the racket. Either alteration increases the effective hitting zone on the racket face by as much as 4 times. In addition, Dr. Bruce Elliott, an Australian sports scientist, showed in 1980 that the wider rackets (as compared to the old elliptical, smaller rackets) were able to absorb the vibrations produced by off-center impacts both toward the sides and toward the ends of the racket face. Even with all this supporting information favoring the larger racket head design, these frames still come under fire when discussed among advanced players. They get power from the rackets but are concerned with control problems during a match. Dr. Elliott also found that these larger rackets produce a higher ball velocity, but there is still the question of ball control and the specific needs of each player.

Selecting a Racket Based on Your Needs

Skilled tennis players should be extremely aware of their equipment's performance relative to their personal needs and game style. As I have discussed, your racket needs depend upon whether you play a baseline game or whether you serve and volley. The trend of consumer usage is to use a stiffer frame in a wide body design. Laboratory studies and play tests have shown the beneficial effects of these rackets, and the industry is answering the demands of players to develop new technology. With the increased hitting zone and increased attempts at developing control with the wide body rackets, players are quickly shifting their interests toward the wide body frames. Additionally, the design and materials of the new rackets are more forgiving for those who are afflicted with arm troubles. People in the industry still believe that graphite dampens the vibrations of impact more than most other materials, so unless technology changes drastically, the graphite composites are still the way to go for efficiency of shock control.

String Types and Tensions

Once you've decided what racket type and flexibility will be most appropriate for you, you must make the final decision about your racket: What string and what tension will best fit your needs? Research during the last decade revealed a lot about strings and tensions that should help you make your decisions. When you walk into a tennis pro shop and ask what types of string the tennis professional uses, are you ready for the possible answers the pro could give? The response could range from a simple recommendation of gut or nylon strings to a discussion of the string's gauge (or thickness) and the variety of synthetics, colors, compositions, and prices from different manufacturers. A lot of research is going into the phenomena involved in string design and function, and it will probably go on indefinitely (just like racket research and development). We can, however, examine what is known about racket strings and give you some idea of what to look for when selecting a string type and tension.

String Type

Let's begin by discussing what sport science has shown us about string types.

Gut is manufactured from the smooth muscle portion of sheep or beef intestine. It is elastic and resilient because it contains a percentage of fat from the animal's natural fiber. Once extracted from the animal, gut undergoes a thorough chemical process of washing, bleaching, twisting, drying, and refining to ensure strength and uniformity. Some gut string is then waterproofed to give it a longer life (especially in high humidity). Once it's installed in your racket, gut is lively and more resilient than most synthetics.

Other types of string include nylon, artificial gut, graphite string, and oil-filled string, which are synthetic. This proliferation of string varieties only adds to the significant problem encountered by most players: How is one to select a string type?

It all depends on what you want from the string. For example, if playability is crucial to you, then you may not find a very durable string that meets your needs. Thinner gauges of string are livelier and can impart more ball spin but will likely break sooner. If cost is important, nylon is a good choice; it's inexpensive, durable, and long lasting. Many string manufacturers claim that their synthetic products play like gut. Although this is possible, it's not probable. It is extremely difficult to produce a string that behaves exactly like natural gut. However, who knows what the future holds for developing a string for a specific racket frame that duplicates the action of gut at impact.

Player evaluations have shown gut to provide better control, higher resultant ball velocities, lower vibration levels to the hand, and improved overall playability when compared to other string types. In addition, some Australian scientists (Ellis, Elliott, & Blanksby, 1978) found that tests on ball velocities off rackets strung with either gut or nylon at the same tension favored the gut string. However, the most recent research in this area has found that the impact depends not only on the string type but also its tension and the racket head size (Groppel, Shin, Thomas, & Welk, 1987). Other studies by Elliott have been conducted to analyze the effects on ball velocity resulting from different tensions of gut vs. nylon. He found that regardless of whether gut or nylon was used, ball velocity decreased when string tension went from 50 pounds to 65 pounds. However, when comparing gut string to nylon at the same levels of tension, he concluded that ball velocities following impact with gut string were superior.

String Tensions

For years, average recreational players were told to string their rackets with nylon at 55 pounds tension. It was thought that this string type and tension would produce optimum playability regardless of game style and would give the racket a healthy life span. Until the early 1980s advanced players were told to string their rackets looser for more control and tighter for more velocity. That thinking has gone completely out the window! Today's tennis players have a myriad of string types and tensions to choose from and, with the aid of research in this area in addition to the dissemination of information from the United States Racket Stringers Association, can more easily select what they personally need. But, imagine the problems of tournament players in the late 70s or early 80s when they read that Borg strung his rackets (the old Donnay rackets with the small racket head) at 80 pounds and was often awakened at night by the "ping" heard as strings broke from the high tension. The next day these players could read about McEnroe stringing his rackets (also the small racket head popular at that time) at about 48 pounds. How could they decide what to do when the two best players in the world strung their equipment so differently? The answer is that world-class players string their rackets based on their personal needs, so why shouldn't you?

The effect of varying string tensions should be important to skilled players wanting to improve. This is so evident on the pro tour that most of the athletes consult with professional stringers who customize the weight, balance, and stringing of their rackets. The tension used by a player can have a tremendous effect on shot velocity and control. In 1983, my colleagues and I conducted a study to examine these effects. As balls were fired against a fixed racket, we used films taken at 500 frames per second to determine the ratio of ball velocity after and before impact. This was done for the same racket strung with nylon at four different tensions (40, 50, 60, and 70 pounds).

From Table 2.1, you can see that a progression of ratios exists from 40 pounds to 70 pounds, with 40 pounds producing the highest ball

Table 2.1   The Effects of String Tension on Postimpact Ball Velocity

String tension (lb)	Average ratio* of $\dfrac{\text{postimpact ball velocity}}{\text{preimpact ball velocity}}$
40 ($n = 10$)[a]	.503
50 ($n = 10$)	.482
60 ($n = 10$)	.467
70 ($n = 10$)	.463

*The higher this ratio, the higher the rebound velocity relative to the ball velocity before impact.

[a]$n = 10$ refers to the 10 trials that were measured at each tension.

velocities. In the early 1980s, this research (along with supporting research from others) put a new perspective on the connection between string tension and ball velocity: The looser the strings (within reason), the higher the ball velocity after impact. One explanation was that the lower the string tension, the more the strings will deflect on impact and the less energy will be absorbed from the ball, which will cause the ball to leave with a faster rebound velocity. That is, the ball will deform less and lose less energy. Subsequently, the ball will rebound with more energy and will have a higher velocity. Another explanation, given by Dr. Howard Brody, was that the larger the portion of energy maintained in the strings, the greater the effect on ball rebound velocity, provided that the time of ball contact with the strings matched the time of string deflection and repositioning. Brody felt that a trampoline effect may then occur as some of the energy stored in the strings during impact is returned to the ball, thus increasing the rebound velocity. As you will soon see, Dr. Brody was right on target when he discussed the string deflection and repositioning.

Velocity must be used with optimal control to play highly skilled tennis. To study the effects of string tension on control, I continued these studies into the mid-1980s by filming impacts at 4,500 frames per second with the same racket at the different string tensions shown in Table 2.1 to see how long the ball stayed on the strings. Table 2.2 shows that the ball stayed on the strings longer (albeit only fractions of milliseconds) at the lower string tension. This research has been supported in subsequent studies, but what does this have to do with control?

One explanation has been that an increase in string tension causes the ball to be flattened out during impact. This flattening out, in turn, causes

Table 2.2   The Effects of String Tension on Contact Duration

Tension (lb)	Contact duration (ms)
40	4.08
50	4.07
60	4.05
70	3.82

an embedding of the strings into the nap of the tennis ball. The greater the embedding of the ball, the greater the control. Although this theory of the ball embedding into the strings has come under some heat recently, a second cause might be that a greater trampoline effect occurs at lower string tensions and that the ball is on the racket face longer. Therefore, when a ball is hit off-center (as most are) the racket has more time to rotate in reaction to the impact and send the ball off in an errant direction. This latter explanation is the one I find more likely.

Other Scientific Information Regarding Type and Tension

Still not satisfied with the understanding we had about string types and tensions, my colleagues and I continued our investigations into the phenomena surrounding racket strings. In 1987 we completed a study to examine the effects of gut and nylon strings that were strung in midsized and oversized rackets at string tensions of 40, 50, 60, 70, and 80 pounds. The results were very intriguing in that we found no linear progression (as in the previous study) in the relationship between string tension and impact. This is the area in which Dr. Brody seemed to be right about how string deflection and racket vibration (or oscillation) affected impacts. Figures 2.4a and b show that gut and nylon behave similarly but not in the linear fashion you might expect. During the investigation the peak ball velocity for gut in oversized rackets occurred at 40 pounds, with tests at 50 and 60 pounds showing similar ball velocities. A decrease in ball velocity was seen at 70 pounds, with a subsequent increase at 80 pounds. For nylon in the oversized rackets, the highest ball velocities were seen at 40 pounds, with linear decreases to 70 pounds and an increase at 80 pounds. In the midsized rackets, gut demonstrated the highest ball velocity at 60 pounds, with the second highest peak at 40 pounds. Nylon in the midsized rackets had the highest ball velocities at 50 pounds, with a slight increase from 70 to 80 pounds. It basically seems that each racket has vibration (or harmonic action) that is specific to its design. When you

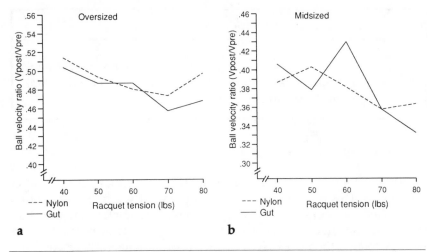

Figure 2.4   Note the effects of gut and nylon on ball velocity in oversized (a) and midsized (b) rackets. *Note*. From Groppel et al. (1987, p. 42). Copyright 1987 by Human Kinetics Publishers, Inc. Reprinted by permission.

string your racket so that the deflection of the string matches that of the racket, it's probable that you are optimizing your equipment to work for you and not against you.

Other variables were examined in this study and another study was completed in 1987, but these results are outside the scope of this book. If you are interested in this information, you can read the journal articles in which they appeared (Groppel et al., 1987a) or you can contact the U.S. Racket Stringers Association, P.O. Box 40, Del Mar, CA, 92014.

Recommendations for Selecting Type and Tension

If you have the time and money, you can certainly try several different types of strings at different tensions. However, because that isn't very realistic, you should probably work with the professional at your tennis pro shop (or consult with someone else who is also a competent stringer) about what strings are available and what would be cost-effective for you. Be sure to string your racket within the manufacturer's recommended ranges, because manufacturers conduct almost all the necessary experiments on their own products and determine where the optimal string tensions are for each racket. Going outside of these recommended tensions could place you in a situation in which your expensive racket isn't working for you properly simply because you have not matched the string tension with the racket mechanics of movement during impact.

Dr. Jack's Tennis Tips

As you develop your game, don't get too hung up on using expensive string in your racket. Most nylons are quite good for development; you can change to gut later.

The Racket's Grip Size

Another factor that you need to consider before buying your new racket is grip size. This is a serious component of racket selection that is often overlooked by tennis players. They often try a couple of grip sizes that feel good and then usually select the smaller grip size because of the whippy feeling the racket gives them. This is a dangerous practice, because the smaller the grip size, the tighter you must squeeze the grip to maintain racket control at impact. The tighter you squeeze the racket, the more fixed your hand becomes to the racket and thus the greater the transmission of force from the racket to the hand, wrist, forearm, and elbow. Therefore, if you are a player who likes the whippy feeling provided by a smaller grip, you may be asking for trouble. One of the most commonly accepted methods to determine the proper grip size is to measure the distance from the middle palm line of the hand to the end of your ring finger (Figure 2.5). Dr. Nirschl, the orthopedic surgeon mentioned earlier in this chapter, developed this method. The measurement is the actual grip size he recommends for players. (Figure 2.5 is not drawn to scale; it is included only for illustrative purposes.)

Your Tennis Shoes and You

Few people realize that the average person takes almost 20,000 steps per day and that with each step, a force of about 120 percent of the body's weight is transmitted through the foot to the ground. Imagine the enormous percentages of body weight transmitted when running, then consider what these numbers become for the quick starts and stops required in tennis. Consider that the foot contains some 26 bones along with tiny muscles and a mass of connective tissue. Slam all of that into the ground for 3 hours a day on the practice court and it's no wonder a skilled tennis player may have sore feet.

The footwork required in tennis is unlike that in most other sports: quick starts in all directions, quick stops from all directions, jumping at

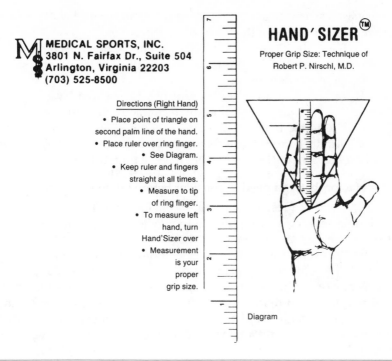

MEDICAL SPORTS, INC.
3801 N. Fairfax Dr., Suite 504
Arlington, Virginia 22203
(703) 525-8500

HAND′ SIZER™

Proper Grip Size: Technique of
Robert P. Nirschl, M.D.

Directions (Right Hand)

• Place point of triangle on
second palm line of the hand.
• Place ruler over ring finger.
• See Diagram.
• Keep ruler and fingers
straight at all times.
• Measure to tip
of ring finger.
• To measure left
hand, turn
Hand'Sizer over
• Measurement
is your
proper
grip size.

Diagram

Figure 2.5   This is one of the more contemporary methods used in selecting a proper grip size (Courtesy of Medical Sports, Inc.).

different angles (e.g., straight up versus angled backward), landing, and twisting. This myriad of maneuvers is further complicated by

• the existence of approximately 16 different tennis court surfaces,
• various climate conditions (e.g., weather and humidity levels), and
• dramatic court surface temperature changes relative to altitude, climate, and season.

All of these factors may affect the friction (traction) between a shoe and surface, and they make the selection of a tennis shoe an important one.

Research on Tennis Shoes

Tennis shoes have not endured the same drastic developmental changes as rackets, but there are still some very interesting trends in technology taking place in the industry. The most innovative trends of the 1980s were both accomplished by Nike: the air sole and the 3/4-top shoe. The air sole was designed to aid the tennis player (and runner) with cushioning to reduce the forces to the lower body. Nike went to great lengths in the research and development laboratory to ensure that the combination of cushioning achieved by the air sole and the stability of the shoe's support system enabled the athlete to play with comfort and endurance.

The 3/4-top shoe was an incredible adventure—one that I was involved with from Day 1. Many think that the technology that created the 3/4-top court shoe added to the tremendous marketing feat, but the way the shoe was introduced to tennis was an accident. Not to say that it would have never happened; the shoe would have definitely been used by tennis players sooner or later, but the following event that took place merely caused this to happen faster.

In 1982, I was requested on behalf of Nike to travel to San Francisco for a filming session with John McEnroe. When I arrived at the hotel, I was met by the tennis promotion manager and two of Nike's engineers to discuss the events for the next couple of days. Early the next day, we met John in one of the banquet rooms of the hotel and took photographs and plaster casts of his feet to appropriately understand his foot structure. Then, it was off to the courts where he played a couple of practice sets while I took high-speed films (at about 100 frames per second) to examine his footwork and attempt to determine how his footwear could be better designed.

The films were developed overnight and the next morning the Nike engineers and I went over the films. What we saw was amazing! When John hopped off the ground (as any player does when anticipating the opponent's shot), his feet angled down slightly (again, just as any player's do). However, when he landed, he did not correct his foot position as readily as he should have. This is definitely not to say that he had a problem with footwork, but rather he was basically too quick for his own feet! Upon landing, his foot position would correct naturally, but sometimes he would land improperly and turn his ankle.

Later that morning we discussed the results of the filming with John and allowed him to sift through about 20 different styles of shoes to select a pair or a couple of pairs that felt good to him and seemed to give him additional support. As John went through all the different pairs of shoes, it didn't seem that any were to his liking. I saw one of the engineers take a pair out of the box and throw them in a corner of the room (I found out later that they were an out-of-line 3/4-top racquetball model that wasn't supposed to be in the box of shoes for John's selection). This discarding action caught John's eye, and (you guessed it) he wanted to see that pair and try them on. He like them and wanted to practice in them that day. We filmed John again and had the films developed overnight.

The films showed that John's movement problem was corrected with these shoes. Many theories could be put forth to explain why the shoes work, but this is the one I feel is true. Although the sidewalls of the shoes do not cross the total ankle joint, they do come right up to it. As John dropped his foot when he left the ground, there was slight pressure against the side of the ankles. The pressure, albeit minimal, caused John to correct his foot position while still airborne and allowed him to land properly.

Factors to Consider When Selecting Tennis Shoes

You should consider many factors when purchasing a pair of tennis shoes. I'm sure you are aware of your specific shoe size, the style you want, and the comfort you expect. However, what entails a perfect shoe fit for a tennis player? Should your style of play affect your shoe selection? Do you consider what court surface you play on and how your choice might affect your performance? How do you evaluate the construction of a shoe and how your foot structure should affect your purchase? The skilled tennis player must confront these issues. The shoes you select will not only affect your quality of play but they may also dictate how long you play the game.

Your Game Style

Let's first consider style of play in your selection of a tennis shoe. Many players are baseliners, whether they hit relentless offensive ground strokes or retrieve and hit moonballs. These players' feet, obviously, encounter a great deal of lateral (to the outside) and medial (to the inside) forces as they push off sideways for a shot or try to catch themselves and change direction. This is not to say players shouldn't worry about forward (anterior) or rear (posterior) forces, but their major support needs will be in the sidewalls of a shoe. The serve-and-volley player also exerts a great deal of sidewall force in pushing off to volley, but this player will also generate very high levels of forward forces into the shoe's toe box when approaching the net. If a serve-and-volleyer wears a shoe that doesn't fit properly, it's possible for the foot to slide forward in the shoe and cause what is known as black toe: a discoloration of the toe due to bruising.

Court Surface

Another external factor besides style of play may affect your decision in selecting a tennis shoe: the court surface. How the shoe sole interacts with the court surface could definitely dictate your caliber of play. For example, if you play on a hard court wearing shoes designed to slide on clay you may not be able to change directions quickly enough, which would risk your safety as well as detract from your game.

Whether or not shoe sole patterns affect the traction between a shoe sole and court surface has generated great controversy. The next time you are in a shoe store, look at the soles of various tennis shoes. You may see wavy lines, Z-patterned lines, concentric circles, uneven circular projections, or combinations of these sole patterns. Some manufacturers have exhaustively studied the interaction of shoe soles and court surface and have tailored their shoe soles to specific court surfaces, so be sure to read the company's literature to be sure your shoe meets your needs.

Shoe Construction

Through the analysis of high-speed films, researchers have determined that most foot striking patterns in tennis involve heel strike (regardless of skill level), the movement of force along the lateral aspect of the shoe sole, and the transmission of that force across to the ball of the foot. This reveals several things to the prospective buyer. First, the construction of the heel cup should be near to formfitting; it should be snug but not constricting. This prevents the foot from slipping out of the shoe and also helps to distribute impact forces more evenly. Second, a snug heel cup seems to be the most important factor in preventing the foot from sliding forward inside the shoe. Also, a rounded outer heel seems to be more beneficial than a square heel construction. The square heel, or one that is right-angled with an abrupt edge, may cause the foot to actually slap the ground after going over the edge of the shoe sole, but a round heel allows the foot to make contact in a smoother and more controlled manner. A soft, pliable, molded heel will also absorb shock better.

Shoe soles must cushion and endure! Some shoes are made from a material designed to do both. Others are constructed of two materials: a cushioned midsole and a harder, more durable outer sole. Dr. Robert Simpson (1982) feels that a polyurethane sole of two thicknesses (a spongy white inner sole and a pliable, but more firm, outer sole) is best. To go a step further, some companies have incorporated into their tennis shoes an air sole that will provide even more cushioning. With proper support and cushioning in this area, the likelihood of foot, lower leg, and knee trauma is lessened.

Shock absorption and support continue from the heel area through the midfoot. To test for midfoot flexibility, flex the sole in the middle. Try to avoid the two extremes: a stiff shoe and a shoe that is too pliable. Too much rigidity absorbs little shock, whereas too much pliability provides little support. This flexion test, though simple, can reveal striking differences among shoe styles.

The force of foot impact moves through the midfoot to the forefoot. Because the body is beginning its push-off at this point and may be twisting over the forefoot to change direction, this area of shoe design is crucial. The greatest pressure may be over the ball of the foot, so you should examine how well that area of the shoe sole is reinforced. In Figure 2.6 you can see what happens to the ball of the foot as a skilled player maneuvers to hit a shot. Again, this area of the shoe should not be too rigid because a great deal of force is encountered in the forefoot. That force could traumatize the foot if poorly distributed and absorbed.

Finally, are you a toe dragger? When you finish serving are there long white lines behind the baseline (Figure 2.7) caused by what used to be part of your shoe? One player on the tour even drags the top of his shoe during ground strokes and goes through the upper before any sign of wear appears on the sole. Not only does this ruin a pair of tennis shoes prematurely, dragging your toe can also affect your balance and your timing. If you drag your toe the best solution is to take some footwork lessons and get out of the habit! It might save you money in the long run. The next best answer, however, is to purchase a shoe with a reinforced toe. Look for shoes with very sturdy outer soles. Several shoe styles even have a larger than usual toe, usually reinforced with polyurethane or some other synthetic. This added padding will help the shoes last a little longer, but the shoe still will probably die before its time.

Foot Structure

Up to this point, we've discussed shoe selection according to style of play, court surface, support, and cushioning of the foot, as well as

Figure 2.6   Gabriela Sabatini pushes off to explode to her right. The torsion within a shoe is very high at this point.

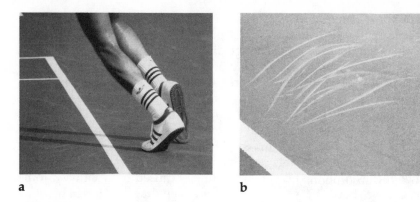

a   b

Figure 2.7   In (a), you can see how many players drag their toes with the trail foot while serving. In (b), you can view the white lines commonly seen behind the baseline of many tennis courts. These lines are caused by the toe of a player's tennis shoe.

wearability, but little has been said regarding basic foot structure and its involvement in shoe selection. I will refer to my work with Dr. Simpson and relate his expertise in podiatry to my study of biomechanics.

We all know our shoe size. When trying on a pair of shoes, we all stand up, lean over, and push the front of the shoe in to determine how much room our toes have. This is a good indicator of the amount of space available in the toe box. You don't want a toe box that constricts, nor do you want a shoe with an oversized toe box that permits free forward migration of the foot. An easy test for this is to stand on the store's carpet and force your foot forward in the shoe. This should indicate how you'll feel later during a tennis match.

Foot width also affects arch support and force distribution. A good rule of thumb while trying on a pair of shoes is to lace both shoes securely, stand up, and let your weight sway to the inside over the arch and then to the outside over the side. If you feel too much pressure from the shoe's own arch, or if you feel any pinching, the shoe is probably too tight; too much foot motion within the shoe may not support your arch adequately and too much pronation (turning outward) can cause severe lower leg and knee trauma.

The heel cup of a shoe should be snug to the foot but not restricting. If it's too tight you may have problems with force distribution and bruising, and if it's too loose, foot control will be poor and blisters may develop. Also, test where the top inner edge of the heel cup contacts your foot. Some people blister easily if the shoe's edge rubs too much against the rear of the foot. If you blister easily, prevention of the problem is the best cure you could have.

Summarizing Shoe Selection

It seems that the old adage "if the shoe fits, wear it" may not necessarily be right. How the shoe fits is what affects your play and the amount of time you can spend on the court. When you select a pair of tennis shoes, bear the following in mind. All tennis players need foot support and cushion, but you may have specific needs based on

- your foot structure,
- comfort,
- shoe weight,
- shock absorption,
- durability,
- reinforced forefoot,
- fit,
- your style of play, or
- the court surface you play on.

Consideration of these factors when selecting your shoes could have a positive effect on how well you play and how long you play.

Dr. Jack's Tennis Tips

Always try on both shoes of a pair and do the same tests discussed here on both. They both must have a good functional fit.

Why So Many Different Tennis Balls?

I thought it was very interesting when the two-tone orange and yellow tennis balls hit the market in the early 1980s. They were advertised as being 23 percent easier to see and were supposed to make a big improvement in your game. However, advertisers never said anything about your opponent also being able to see the ball 23 percent better or mentioned how his or her game would also improve.

Tennis balls are a big part of the market. In recent years the tennis ball industry has accounted for approximately 20 percent of the total money spent by the tennis consumer in the United States. Because that part of the industry is so profitable, many brands of tennis balls exist. Their selection may depend on the court surface to be played on, the altitude, or your duration of play. Most tennis players acknowledge that there is a difference among the various brand names of tennis balls on the market. The differences range from variations in flight and rebound characteristics to the ball's ability to maintain constant characteristics during play (e.g., whether they fluff up or not). Let's discuss some of these differences.

One major identifying characteristic among some brands of tennis balls is whether they are pressurized or not. Nonpressurized balls may be useful at higher altitudes, but you will seldom see them used at major tournaments. The reason is that many skilled players say these balls feel like rocks when they hit the racket. Some authorities even feel that the impact is so heavy that use of these balls could hurt your arm. Little research has been conducted on the nonpressurized ball so none of this information can be verified, but most advanced players prefer playing with pressurized tennis balls

Once a tennis ball is pressurized, it must be placed in a vacuum-sealed container so each ball will maintain its pressure. If the can is properly sealed it makes a short, but loud, hiss when opened. After a pressurized can of balls has been opened each ball will maintain its original rebound characteristics for about a week (Rand, Hyer, and Williams, 1979). After a week of just sitting in an open can the tennis ball will gradually lose its pressure and become dead.

Most pressurized tennis balls are manufactured for use at near-sea-level atmospheric conditions. Those of you who have a chance to play in higher altitudes should be aware that high-altitude balls are made by almost all major manufacturers. In fact, if you try to play a match at a mountain resort using sea-level balls, you are in for a frustrating day because the sea-level balls will tend to sail out of bounds. In contrast, don't take the high-altitude balls home with you or to the beach. These tennis balls are specifically made for use in low-pressure altitudes.

When you make a tennis ball purchase, you might read on the can that it contains balls classified as championship or extra duty. Extra-duty tennis balls have more wool nap on the rubber cover, which allows the ball to have a longer life span. The main disadvantage of these balls is that on a clay surface, and some hard courts, they tend to fluff up and become heavy. Championship balls do not contain as much nap covering and do not fluff up as much. Their main disadvantage is that they won't last as long as some players might like. Most USTA tournaments use the championship ball, introducing new balls at various points in a match because they lose their original characteristics and may become light due to loss of nap.

As you select a tennis ball for competition or practice, consider the court surface and how long you want to use the balls. If you are collecting practice balls, you will probably want to buy extra-duty balls. If you are competing or are practicing on a clay court, you may want to select championship balls. Don't worry about buying a "bad" ball; most tennis ball manufacturers are very involved in quality control.

Dr. Jack's Tennis Tips

I recommend you only use pressurized championship balls as you prepare for tournament play. Very few tournaments use non-pressurized or extra-duty balls. If you have questions about the ball being used at a specific tournament, look closely at the entry form or call the tournament director. Practicing with the tournament ball will help you play well on match day.

NET RESULTS

Always be selective when buying your tennis equipment. It's easy to be swayed into a purchase by salespeople. Don't buy whatever seems to be the most popular brand name. Regardless of the equipment you are looking for, be objective in making your choice. Ask yourself the following questions:

- What are my physical needs (e.g., grip size and foot structure)?
- Does my style of play affect my equipment needs?
- Could this purchase make me a better player?

By being objective in your selection of equipment, you can narrow the choices that will be best for you. Then you can be more subjective by play-testing the equipment to see how it will feel when you use it. By approaching your purchase in this manner, you will get equipment that's best suited to you.

C H A P T E R 3

Footwork Is the Name of the Game

The factor in tennis that most limits players' success is movement. In fact, I feel that it really doesn't matter how great your strokes are if you are not in the right place at the right time. So it's hard for me to understand why players don't spend more time working specifically on movement. Anyone who has taken tennis lessons knows how teaching professionals emphasize footwork and positioning. Yet few athletes truly understand the roles of a ready position, unweighting, response time, and power or how to time a shot that has to be hit on the run. Some tennis players I have worked with are fast in a 20-yard dash, but when I break down their performance I've found that they are really fast from 5 to 15 yards and really slow from 0 to 5 yards. And guess what—the average distance you run for a stroke is 2 to 6 yards. In fact, about 70 percent of the errors that occur in skilled tennis strokes are not due to stroke mechanics per se but to movement.

Your Center of Gravity and Balance

Without good balance, a tennis player is doomed to mediocrity. Balance is controlled by the position of your center of gravity, the central point located slightly above the center of the pelvic region about which the body mass is distributed. Interestingly, the location of your center of gravity changes as your limbs change their positions and when you add extra weight to your hand (i.e., a racket). As you simply place a racket in your hand, your center of gravity shifts slightly in the direction of the racket. If you lift your arm, the center of gravity moves in the same direction. Consider then how the center of gravity shifts position during the countless maneuvers that take place during a match: Every time the positions of the arms and legs change, so does the position of the center of gravity. How you handle these changes dictates how well you maintain your balance during competition.

Line of Gravity and Base of Support

Imagine a line dropped vertically from your center of gravity to the ground. This line of gravity should fall to the ground somewhere over or between your feet. Your feet and the area between them form your base of support. How the line of gravity and your base of support work together will enable you to sprint quickly, maintain balance, or fall down. For example, if you stand at attention with your feet together, the base of support is small. When you spread your feet, the base of support expands and you will become more stable, even though the line of gravity may not move. Optimal balance occurs when the line of gravity falls within the boundaries of the base of support; the nearer the line falls to the center of the base of support, the more stable the player (Figure 3.1). This fine line between balance and imbalance is the key to your success in moving on the court, because once the line of gravity falls outside your base of support, you must either move or fall flat to the court.

To demonstrate the interplay between the line of gravity and the base of support, assume an erect posture with your feet comfortably spread. Without moving your shoulders, lift one foot. If you did this as I explained, I hope your fall to the ground wasn't too painful, because once one foot left the ground, your line of gravity was outside the new base of support (your one foot) and you began to go down. However, if you shifted your shoulders toward your one stable foot, you were able to keep your balance because the line of gravity shifted over the new base.

The falling action created when the line of gravity falls outside the base of support will cause you to start running. The shift from balance to imbalance initiates the sprint. The imbalance forces you to move your

Figure 3.1 As Gabriela Sabatini prepares to serve, you can see that she is
stable; her center of gravity is over the heel of the front foot.

feet to keep from falling, this continual process of balance to imbalance
keeps your body under control as you sprint. The push-off from your
hind foot forces the line of gravity forward over the base of support, and
the opposite leg swings forward, catches the body before it falls, and
then becomes the push-off leg for the next stride.

Just as the position of the center of gravity rises when the arms are
raised, it lowers when the body crouches. The lower your center of gravity, the more stable your body. However, it is possible to crouch too low
when awaiting the opponent's shot. This excessive crouch causes too
much stability, making your response to the opponent's shot slow and
inefficient. This raises the discussion of how your ready position should
look.

The Ready Position and Unweighting

Good footwork begins with the ready position: knees bent slightly,
weight forward on the balls of your feet, body bent slightly forward at
the waist moving your center of gravity lower and forward (ready to
explode in any direction), and racket held directly in front of your body.
Although this ready position is fairly well accepted, some teaching professionals prefer a more general stance, somewhat like a neutral position.

The neutral position really doesn't describe any particular stance such
as the ready position. Because the knees must bend to create movement
regardless of whether they are flexed before the action or not, advocates
of the neutral position ask, Why bend prematurely? They feel that the

issue is whether you are "aware" of the opponent's shot or not. If you are in the neutral position and are properly aware, you will read the opponent's shot and move quickly just as well as a player who assumes an actual ready position stance. Even world-class players, who have already demonstrated their abilities to perform, use different stances to await opponents' shots (Figure 3.2). Therefore, you probably don't need a specific stance to begin with, but you might want to use an actual ready position if it helps you anticipate the opponent's shot.

As soon as you read the opponent's shot, you will unweight. You may have heard this term used in skiing when a skier turns against the snow. Unweighting in tennis simply refers to a lessening of force between a player's shoes and the court surface. Before you prepare to move, the force between your shoes and the court is equal to your body weight. Once you make the decision to move, your knees will quickly flex, decreasing the force between your shoes and the court. Then, as your knees extend to push off, the force between your shoes and the court exceeds your body weight. To see how this works, stand on a bathroom scale and note the reading. Now jump off the scale! You should have seen the needle (or numbers if you have a digital scale) go down as you flexed your knees and then go above your actual weight as you accelerated upward to jump off the scale. This is exactly the process that occurs on the court. Your knees flex, decreasing the force against the court and allowing your feet to change positions, and then forcefully extend to push off. The next step is following the ball to get in position.

a   b

Figure 3.2   Zina Garrison and Boris Becker demonstrate how a player awaits the opponent's shot.

Tracking

The principle of tracking, or visually following the ball's movement and responding to it with your own movement, is an often overlooked aspect of a tennis player's development. Advanced players have probably mastered tracking, but intermediates and beginners always have problems with it. For example, the faster a ball travels toward you, the harder it is to track. Likewise, balls traveling at very low or very high trajectories are also difficult to track.

Depending on your skill level, you can use various drills that employ the tracking skills required to play tennis. If you are a beginner, have someone stand about 5 to 10 feet away from you and toss balls slowly toward you in a small arc. As you increase your success in catching the balls, have the thrower increase the speed and arc of the toss. Once you reach a difficult speed and arc, practice until you can catch the balls easily. Your goal is to recognize the position and velocity of the balls as quickly as possible.

As your skill develops in this area (or if you are already proficient in the drill just described), have your partner toss the balls to different positions, forcing you to change direction and move quickly to get in position to catch the balls. Balls can be tossed wide, short, or behind you as you learn to track and move, much like you must do on the tennis court. Later in this chapter, I will discuss some specific tracking and movement drills that I prescribe to players at all skill levels.

The Unit Turn

Once the ball has left the opponent's racket, it's time to move! The easiest shot to return is one hit very close to you so you don't have to run for it. If the ball comes right to your forehand, for example, the next movement that will occur is the unit turn. Instead of taking the racket back with your arm alone, you take the racket back by movements of the legs, hips, and shoulders. Basically, the body moves as one unit.

As soon as you recognize the direction of the ball off the opponent's racket, you should move the foot closest to the side where the ball is traveling, as you see in Figure 3.3. For example, if you're a right-hander and the ball is coming to your forehand, you will pick up the right foot and point it outward to that side. As this happens, the whole right side of the body, including the racket, rotates around to the right. Done properly, this movement should also cause a slight forward imbalance. Although it is desirable to step toward the ball with the opposite foot (the left in this case), the unit turn also allows for the stroke to be hit

a   b

Figure 3.3   Ivan Lendl and Jennifer Capriati demonstrate how a player uses the unit turn to prepare for a return.

regardless of whether or not you have time to step into the shot. However, if you don't step into the shot, your center of gravity will tend to remain either directly above or behind your feet (instead of slightly forward as it should be) and you will not hit the ball as well as you could.

Moving a Short Distance Laterally

Because the unit turn naturally involves motion to the side, it readily prepares the body for quick lateral movement. The turn enhances two kinds of lateral motion: shuffling the feet sideways and sprinting. First, imagine that the ball is only going to be about 4 feet directly to your right at impact (Figure 3.4). You may not have to sprint, but you will still need to move quickly.

In explaining how to do this, I like to use an analogy from basketball. Picture Michael Jordan playing defense near the basket about 5 feet from his own baseline. He is guarding an opposing player who has the ball. His opponent begins to drive the baseline around him. How will Jordan prevent the player from going around him? Obviously, he won't turn and sprint 5 feet! He will "slide" over to the baseline, cutting off the opponent's path to the basket.

This sliding is accomplished by shuffling the feet side to side very quickly. It's the quickest way to move a very short distance laterally, especially if you are an intermediate player or below. You see, once you

Figure 3.4 This athlete demonstrates how to move quickly to the side. Notice the shuffling of the feet (a, b, and c), which allows him to move more rapidly than would a complete striding movement.

shuffle a couple of steps, you are still in a ready position (Figure 3.5) and can perform the unit turn, rotate, and step into the shot. This makes the game very easy, because you never have to judge where your body is relative to the ball when you have to move a short distance to the side. If you are a skilled player, however, you must learn to "explode" toward almost every ball. If the ball is only a couple of steps away you can shuffle, but seldom will you be able to do this if you are playing another skilled player; he or she is not going to hit the ball that close to you that often.

a   b   c

Figure 3.5   This player demonstrates how to shuffle laterally and then use the unit turn to prepare the racket.

When the ball is farther than a few feet from you, you must definitely explode to the ball. The unit turn allows your foot to turn out in the right direction, and the forward imbalance caused by the unit turn enables you to complete the explosion. When viewing any great mover on the tennis court, watch what he or she does. The first movement is to drive toward the ball, sprint, and then stutter step to gain the perfect stroke position.

Dr. Jack's Tennis Tips

A good cue that might help you with your footwork is to think of attacking the ball with your feet. As the ball approaches you, think of aggressively moving to get in position as quickly as possible.

How the foot closest to the side where the ball is traveling moves has recently come under great discussion. Some feel that a "gravity step" should be employed by the athlete to gain the driving action toward the ball. This gravity step occurs like this: Once the player recognizes the ball moving to his or her right (for example), the right foot actually pulls back under the body and drives the body toward the ball. This action is somewhat like the pawing action a runner uses when his or her foot extends forward and then comes back under the body, seeming to pull the body over the pawing foot. A problem I see with this action is that few athletes can accomplish it without forcing the center of gravity to rise upward as the leg is pulled under the body. I realize that the athlete is supposed to "fall" in the direction of the ball, but this may be difficult for some players to do. I prefer to teach tennis players a combination of what baseball experts call a jab step and then a crossover.

In the early 1980s I had the fortune to work with the baserunning coach for the Chicago White Sox, Dave Nelson. Dave, who has gone on to direct the minor league system for the Oakland A's and who now works with the Cleveland Indians, was a major league all-star player and at one time led the American League in stolen bases, so he was considered an expert at what he did and what he coached. We spent two entire seasons filming the best base runners in the American League, trying to determine the best start technique for a base runner attempting to steal a base. The big controversy in the major leagues was whether a runner should use a jab step, which resembles the unit turn we have defined, or whether the right foot (the foot closest to second base) should pivot and the left should cross over.

Many of the runners in our study used a gravity step to accelerate toward second base. In fact, once the study was completed, the results were obvious: The fastest base runners used a combination of both the jab and crossover. They first jabbed the right foot out to the side and then pulled it under to "paw" the ground while simultaneously driving with the left leg, which immediately crossed over to assume the sprinting action. Bear in mind, however, that a base runner knows he must sprint full out toward the next base. Tennis players will naturally learn to do this. This is how I feel tennis players should learn to move: Jab with the foot closest to where the ball is headed, and then cross over to sprint. Yes, it's possible that the gravity step will be faster for some, but I truly feel that players must learn to move by jabbing and then crossing over just like the base runner.

Dr. Jack's Tennis Tips

A cue you can use to improve your movement is "Ready, read, react!" Make sure you are always ready as the opponent begins to hit the ball; then immediately focus on the ball and read what has happened during the opponent's contact with the ball; and finally, react to move. Pretend your legs are elastic and have the feeling of explosiveness. This awareness training has helped a lot of players in their on-court movement. In fact, it was the same cue used to help the players on the 1988 U.S. Olympic volleyball team as they prepared to return an opponent's spike.

Hitting on the Run

Skilled players must be able to hit a shot on the run. While being a crowd pleaser in itself, it is also one of the most exhilarating feelings in tennis to be running full tilt and hit a down-the-line passing shot for a clear winner. However, even as thrilling as it is, that shot has to be one of the toughest in tennis because of the footwork, body positioning, timing, and racket work necessary to make it successful.

The key point to remember about hitting on the run is to be as balanced as possible. Sometimes body stability is very difficult to master, especially if you are not accustomed to your opponent's hitting short or angled shots. In situations like this, hitting on the run is a must and balance is the least of a player's worries. However, many shots hit on the run aren't necessary; this may happen because of laziness, poor timing, inaccurate judgment of the ball off the opponent's racket, or just the desire to hit a crowd pleaser. When you watch a player who seems to be hitting a great number of balls while sprinting, watch his or her body positioning and footwork. The footwork might be a little lazy, even slow motion, at the start of the movement toward the ball. Then, as the ball gets closer to where contact will occur, the player suddenly accelerates and ends up lurching at the ball. Players who do this are timing their bodies, not their strokes, to the position of ball contact, making a balanced shot almost impossible. This causes a hurried, cramped swing that often has poor results. To prevent (or correct) this problem, you need to get to the court position where the ball will be hit slightly before the ball arrives. When you arrive early at the site of ball contact, you will more easily achieve upper body balance, timing, and accuracy of the stroke.

If you have to hit a ball on the run, how should you get to it properly? Many players might answer, Run as hard as you can (and sometimes that's exactly what you have to do)! However, try as they might, some players don't know how to run correctly when they have rackets in their hands. For example, many tennis players feel they must run with the rackets back in preparation to swing. If you are in the early stages of learning to move with your racket, maybe you will have to run with the racket back, but if you're beyond that stage, forget it! The human body was not made to run with the arm extended backward while holding a racket. It causes you to be at least twice as slow.

A well-known track coach once told me that sprinters were only as fast as their arms would let them be. Basically, the arms must pump just as hard as the legs to help the player accelerate. This arm action assists in coordinating the quick action of the legs. The racket arm can be held in close just the same as if there were no racket in the hand. Just be careful that when you begin pumping your racket arm to help accelerate yourself, you don't crack yourself in the head with your racket!

Swinging the Racket When on the Run

The key to running with the racket is knowing when to initiate the back-swing. Many players go through total dysfunction when trying to com-bine all these movements. To be the most balanced, your opposing limbs (e.g., left leg and right arm) should move in synchrony. Picture sprinting to the side for a forehand passing shot down the line. Try to run slightly forward, as the player in Figure 3.6 demonstrates. By running forward, you will have forward linear momentum toward the point of impact (if you move directly to the side, all of your momentum is to the side and if you move backward, all of your momentum is backward as well).

During your stride, as your foot nearest the ball contacts the court (the left foot for a right-handed player), your racket arm should begin moving backward into its slightly circular backswing. The swing continues and as the hind foot pushes off the ground (the right foot for a right-handed player), the hips and trunk rotate slightly, transferring force from the

a

b

c

d

Figure 3.6   This player shows how to time your stroke to the point of impact. Notice in (d) how he is "set" and balanced for the forward swing.

ground out to the racket arm for an effective ball contact well in front of the body.

Dr. Jack's Tennis Tips

Sometimes you won't gauge the distance between your body and the ball properly. When this happens, try stutter stepping as you near the ball. This stutter stepping will enable you to gain control of your body and get into position the most efficient way.

There are obviously other ways to hit a ball on the run, but this technique allows for total use of the linear and angular momentum. The timing for certain shots may not permit this movement coordination either, but if time and body position allow, this method is the most efficient.

Dr. Jack's Tennis Tips

When moving to hit a ball (especially a passing shot), try to cut the ball off by moving slightly forward. This enables you to have forward linear momentum and means you will not have to swing as forcefully to hit the shot. Also, be sure to keep your upper body under control when initiating your swing on the run.

Returning a Ball Hit Right at You

Just as some people have trouble hitting on the run, others seem to have a phobia for balls coming right at them. They often panic because they don't know what to do. This occurs most often at the beginning level of tennis, but it can also be seen at the skilled level. A beginner or advanced beginner can be at the baseline (with the opponent also at the baseline at least 78 feet away) and see the ball traveling toward him or her. Instead of getting out of the ball's flight path, the player stays put and ends up scooping the racket in front of the body just trying to keep the ball in play. This embarrassing situation is the result of either poor concentration or poor footwork. When a skilled player gets jammed by a ball, it's usually caused by poor concentration or simply laziness in preparing for the shot.

Regardless of the reason for getting jammed by an opponent's shot, there is a simple philosophy that works all the time—*get out of the way*! As simplistic—and probably ridiculous—as this sounds, it's true. The pros are usually the best at moving away from approaching balls. Their footwork is not necessarily continuous (in other words, they're not jumping around all the time) but as their opponents prepare to hit the shot, they are ready to pounce. As soon as they recognize the ball heading toward them, they will immediately move to the side into position for their own strokes. As they move to the side, they keep their centers of gravity over their feet to stay balanced to hit controlled returns.

This is where less skilled players can get into trouble. Knowing how far to move to the side is crucial. If the movement is too far away from where the ball will be hit, the player is always stretching, and if the movement isn't far enough, the swing will be cramped. Experience at moving away from the ball is important, but it doesn't take too much practice to learn the proper action. It's usually a matter of focusing on what you must do the first few times, practicing it several more times once you've got it down, and then using it in competition.

Recovery After a Shot

Often you will find yourself returning a ball that has taken you outside the court boundaries. Even if the return only takes you to one of the sidelines, you have to recover toward a strategic court position. This recovery step is vital to the development of your on-court coverage. A problem encountered by many athletes is that they focus so hard on returning to a strategic court position that they don't hit the shot well. In fact, some players can be seen recovering before they hit the ball!

Your first goal is to hit the ball well. Once you've ensured a solid impact, then recover. For example, your body should be well controlled at ball contact. There should be no extraneous movement that might hamper the stroke. Now you can square around to the net and begin recovering.

After a player hits an aggressive forehand, for example, it's common to see the trail leg rotate around to square the athlete's body to the net. The player immediately brakes by planting the trail leg and pushes off to return toward a strategic court position (notice I did not say the player always returns to the middle of the baseline, because the fact remains that sometimes it's impossible to get all the way back to the center of the court). Once you are sure your shot will be or has been hit with maximum control, you can swing your trail leg around and push off back toward the center (Figure 3.7). If you cannot make it back to the center of the court, be sure to square off to the opponent before he or she makes

Figure 3.7   Jennifer Capriati demonstrates the type of shot where a recovery step should be performed. Her right foot will swing around after ball contact, plant against the court and push off to help her gain a strategic court position.

contact with the ball. If you're still heading toward the center of the baseline when the ball is contacted, you are easy prey to a ball hit behind you.

Dr. Jack's Tennis Tips

Remember that when you are recovering to a strategic court position, and just before the opponent swings at the ball, square off to the opponent so you can retrieve a ball hit behind you. Because of your momentum it will be easy to continue running toward the center of the baseline, but if you're headed that way and the ball is hit behind you, the point is over in favor of your opponent!

Open- and Closed-Stance Ground Strokes

Many players don't need to worry about a recovery step because they are often already opened up when they hit the ball. There are many theories, both positive and negative, about open-stance ground strokes. As a rule, there's nothing wrong with an open-stance stroke, provided the player has time to get set and hit the ball correctly. Only certain strokes, however, allow usage of an open stance. For example, have you ever wondered why the forehand is so often hit with an open stance?

How often do you see a one-handed backhand hit from an open stance? Let's analyze these various ground strokes to determine some answers.

If a right-handed player stands facing the net awaiting the opponent's shot and the opponent strikes a ball toward his or her forehand side, the player may only have to sidestep, rotate the body, and swing, hence the open-stance forehand. There will be little transfer of body weight forward; only body rotation will allow the athlete to take a sufficient backswing and swing effectively. This will be discussed in depth in the next chapter.

However, seldom will you see a one-handed backhand hit from an open stance. If a ball is hit to the player's backhand side, the racket is on the side of the body opposite the position of the ball. Therefore, the player must reach across his or her body to prepare the racket for the return. Imagine the contortions a player would have to go through to sidestep toward the ball and hit an open-stance, one-handed backhand. Therefore, I recommend you use the orthodox, closed-stance, one-handed backhand seen in Figure 3.8. As may be evident, good footwork is essential to adequately position your body sideways for the stroke.

Footwork is also necessary for a successful two-handed backhand, but what about an open-stance two-hander? You will actually see more open-stance, two-handed backhands than one-handers, but why? One reason may come from some of the coaching literature of the 1970s, a time when the two-handed backhand became so popular. Many of the authors

a   b   c

Figure 3.8 This tennis player demonstrates the proper movements when hitting an effective one-handed backhand drive.

referred to the two-handed backhand (of a right-handed player) as being similar to hitting a left-handed forehand. They implied that because the left hand is placed closer to the racket face, it is the more important of the two hands. Whether you believe this rationale or not, it may help to explain the possibility of hitting the two-handed backhand with an open stance. Saying that the stroke resembles a left-handed forehand (of a right-handed player) implies that shoulder rotation (to bring the left hand around) is the dominant producer of force to swing the racket. That would mean that the body could be open to swing the racket as long as the right hand was still holding the racket as a minor producer of force and for additional racket control. An effective two-hander can be hit so it looks like the stroke is hit with an open stance. As you can see from Figure 3.9, some players will set up to swing in a half-open stance (stepping more toward the net instead of directly toward the ball), and as they initiate the swing, their trunks will rotate toward the ball along with a recovery step, which makes it seem like the player has actually swung with a completely open stance.

No matter how unique or spectacular you think an open-stance ground stroke is, most players should always try to get into position as quickly as possible and step into the shot. This method helps to improve footwork and enables players to hit with better control. The player who steps into the shot will also be able to reach farther with more control; the player using the open-stance stroke must either get slightly closer to the ball for an effective impact or move quicker to get in position for the

Figure 3.9 The figure drawing, taken from films shot at 100 frames per second, shows how Bjorn Borg hit his effective half-open stance two-handed backhand drive so well.

swing. Sometimes, however, there isn't time to stop and step into the shot; the open-stance shot may be all you have.

Regardless of whether you prefer open- or closed-stance shots, there are several things to remember when working on your body positioning. As you await the opponent's shot, try to keep your feet moving so you don't get caught flat-footed. I tell my players to have "happy feet" as they get prepared for a return. That doesn't mean you jump around like a jackrabbit, but when the opponent begins his or her forward swing, take a very short hop to set your leg muscles for movement to the ball. This hop should be timed so that you land at exactly the same time the opponent hits the ball. Your first movement should then be a unit turn to the side. If you don't have to sprint for the ball, shuffle your feet and get prepared as early as possible. If you must sprint toward the ball, try to get there early so your upper body can be as stable as possible. Avoid hitting on the run whenever you can.

As far as hitting with an open or closed stance, you can do whatever you want. Remember, however, that most players who hit from an open stance don't do so because it might be more effective, but simply because they're lazy. To help you with your movement, I'll share some of the movement drills we use with our players at Harry Hopman/Saddlebrook International Tennis.

How to Improve Your Movement

You can use numerous drills that will improve your on-court movement. These drills have been designed with the assistance of my colleague, Mike Nishihara (assistant director of sports and health development at Saddlebrook Resort). Mike conducts movement lessons for many students in the player development program at Harry Hopman/Saddlebrook International Tennis. Although I may be a bit biased, we have had excellent success in helping tennis players with response time, acceleration, speed, agility, dynamic balance, and coordination.

The key to the success of these drills is that we have designed them to be specific to tennis. There are no lights, bells, or whistles for the player to respond to; the ball is the only cue we use as a stimulus. The movements I will describe have been designed based on research by my colleagues or by other U.S. researchers in addition to some of the work done by the German Tennis Federation. To help you understand why these drills will enable you to move better on the court, we will discuss some of these research findings.

The average distance moved per stroke in a competition between two skilled males is about 2 meters on hard court and 4 meters on clay. In a two-set match, these players will run a total distance of 1,648 meters (a little over 1 mile), and this is spread out over about an hour. Directional changes can range from about 4 to 8 times per point, implying that in competition a skilled player will change direction about every 1.4 to 2.0 seconds.

These data come from video analyses of actual singles matches played between two skilled athletes. It's arguable that data obtained on men's and women's matches would be drastically different, but I speculate that the data will reflect similarities. Yes, the points of some women's matches are longer than those in some men's matches, but I think the match statistics might even out. To demonstrate what I mean, take a look at the data taken from the men's and women's finals from the 1988 U.S. Open Tennis Tournament.

Lendl Versus Wilander

Total points = 325

Time of match = 4 hours, 54 minutes

Average time per point = 12.2 seconds

Average time between serves = 12.1 seconds

Average time between points = 28.3 seconds

Average time per changeover = 128.2 seconds*

Percent points in less than 10 seconds = 59 percent

Percent points in 10 to 20 seconds = 22 percent

Percent points in more than 20 seconds = 19 percent

Graf Versus Sabatini

Total points = 161

Time of match = 1 hour, 41 minutes

Average time per point = 10.8 seconds

Average time between serves = 10.7 seconds

Average time between points = 16.2 seconds

Average time per changeover = 100.1 seconds*

Percent points in less than 10 seconds = 62 percent

Percent points in 10 to 20 seconds = 25 percent

Percent points in more than 20 seconds = 13 percent

(Match statistics reprinted with permission of Dr. Jeff Chandler, the scientist who obtained these data.)

*It is speculated that changeover times were longer than the allowed 90 seconds because the players remained seated in their chairs courtside until the 90 seconds elapsed.

As you can see, the point statistics are similar even though the men played longer and they probably hit the ball harder than did the women. With this is mind, I feel any tennis player, regardless of gender, can benefit from the movement drills I recommend. Please don't use these drills to get in cardiovascular condition—develop a solid aerobic foundation before trying these exercises. And if you have never done exercises like these before or if you have any concerns about doing them, consult your physician about doing them.

As you practice the drills, try to simulate the points and games of an actual match. For example, a point can last anywhere from 5 seconds (I realize if a service winner is hit, the point lasts about .5 seconds) to about 25 or 30 seconds (sometimes longer but this is rare). One study found that the average point on clay between two skilled males was 10 seconds; on hard court it was 5.2 seconds and on grass 2.8 seconds. The average time between points is usually from 16 seconds to a maximum of 30 seconds. After simulating about 10 or 12 points, take a 90-second break from the drills to simulate a changeover. Do these drills twice a week for approximately 20 to 30 minutes. Doing them more often than this will not necessarily bring faster improvement.

Movement Drills for Quicker Footwork

Based on the information presented so far, I feel there are several factors to consider that will make you a faster tennis player:

- how well you see the ball off the opponent's racket,
- how quickly you process the ball's speed, direction, and spin,
- how well you decide what to do relative to moving and depth perception,
- how fast the nerve signal passes from your brain to your leg muscles (I know of no current research that allows me to help you improve this factor!), and, most importantly,
- your first step!

Because the average distance you will move during a stroke is about 4 meters, doesn't it make sense that your first step when moving to the ball is crucial? That's why the keys to these footwork drills involve your moving relative to the ball's motion with your first step.

Ball Reaction Drill. Just like the football defensive back drill you see in pregame warm-ups, this drill requires you to respond to the movement of the ball. A coach or partner holds the ball in clear vision (Figure 3.10). The coach can move the ball in four different directions, to which you must respond. If the ball moves toward you, you must backpedal; if the ball goes to the right or left, you must sideshuffle in the direction of the

Figure 3.10   The coach holds the ball high and well in view of you. As the coach moves the ball, you must react in that direction.

ball; and if the ball moves away from you, you must sprint forward. Try to do about four of these lasting about 10 seconds each (the average time per point) and have about 20 to 25 seconds between each one (the average time between points).

Toss-and-Catch Drill.   The coach or partner stands about 8 to 10 feet in front of you (Figure 3.11). The coach can gently toss a tennis ball to either side of you, in front of you, or behind you. You must react and explode to the ball, catching it (either with one hand or two, depending on how hard you want to work). Immediately upon catching the ball, toss it back to the coach. The coach, always keeping the ball in your sight, immediately tosses the ball to another area. This keeps up for about 10 seconds, then you have 20 to 25 seconds to rest before doing it again. Do this drill about 4 times, bearing in mind that the maximum distance you should run for each ball is about 4 meters.

Roll-and-Catch Drill.   The coach or partner stands about 8 to 10 feet in front of you (Figure 3.12). The coach rolls a tennis ball to either side of or softly in front of you. You must react to the rolling ball, exploding toward the ball to catch it and toss it back to the coach. Upon receiving it, the coach rolls the ball to another area no more than 4 meters away, always ensuring the ball is in your sight. Again, do about 4 of these

Figure 3.11   The coach can toss the ball short, deep, or to either side, forcing you to react in that direction and catch the ball before it bounces.

Figure 3.12   The coach can roll the ball to either side or short, forcing you to react in that direction to retrieve the ball.

lasting about 10 seconds each with a 20- to 25-second rest in between each.

Toss- or Roll-and-Catch Drill.   This is simply a combination of the previous two drills; the coach can either toss the ball or roll it so you must respond to a ball in flight or one on the court's surface. Everything else remains the same as the previous drills.

Hexagon Drill.   This drill uses a six-sided figure with sides of 24 inches and equal angles between sides (Figure 3.13). The hexagon shape allows the player to practice moving in many directions. Begin inside the hexagon, and upon the command of "ready, go!" by the coach or partner (who has a stopwatch), jump from inside the hexagon to outside the hexagon and back inside again, always landing on both feet, and continuing this motion around the hexagon 3 times as quickly as possible without touching a line or missing a movement. You only need to do this a couple of times but be sure to have 30 seconds of rest between trials. This is a great drill for agility, dynamic balance, and coordination.

Figure 3.13   On the command of "Ready, go!" you must hop from inside the hexagon to outside and back in all the way around the hexagon 3 times.

Spider Run.   The backcourt is set up with tennis balls placed at the intersections of the singles sidelines and baseline, intersections of the singles sidelines and service line, and the intersection of the service line and center service line. Begin with one foot on the center mark at the baseline (Figure 3.14). On the command of "ready, go!" by the coach or partner, sprint to the ball on the deuce court side, pick it up, and return it to the center mark. Immediately, sprint to the next ball in a counterclockwise fashion, picking up all the balls and placing them down at the center mark. The coach's role is twofold: to move each ball out of the way as it is set down at the center mark and to use a stopwatch to give you feedback on how well you do. Do not do this more than twice with a 30-second rest between runs.

Figure 3.14   On the command of "Ready, go!" you must sprint to the right, pick up the ball, and return it to the starting position. This continues in a counterclockwise fashion until all balls are gathered.

Alley Lunges and Hops.   These movements simulate the recovery step. Stand on one side of the alley (Figure 3.15) and do 10 lunges from one side of the alley to the other. (Don't be concerned if your legs are short—you don't have to jump completely outside the alley lines.) The first 10 jumps should be lunges that are powerful, yet controlled. Then, rest at least 30 seconds and do 10 hops from one side to the other by doing the same movement, only don't jump as far or as forcefully— movements for the hops should be rapid and controlled.

Eye-Hand Coordination Drills.   Stand about 6 to 8 feet from a wall or backboard. As you face the wall, the coach assumes a position directly behind you (Figure 3.16). As you anticipate the ball going by, the coach tosses a ball against the wall either to your right or left. Your goal is to catch the ball before it flies past you after rebounding against the wall. This drill can be easy at first and then gradually made more difficult by the coach tossing the ball faster, your moving closer to the wall, or both. Do this 8 to 10 times for each side of the body.

Figure 3.15 You must lunge from one side of the alley to the other and re-bound back to the other for the duration of this exercise.

Figure 3.16 Stand about 6 to 8 feet from the wall with the coach behind you. The coach tosses the ball to one side and you must react and catch the ball before it rebounds past.

Partner Quick Hands Drill.   You and your partner stand facing each other about 3 to 4 feet apart. Crouching so each of you can field rolling tennis balls, each person has a ball in his or her right hand. One of you says, "ready, go!" and each person rolls a ball toward the other (Figure 3.17). Immediately upon catching the ball roll it back, and continue this process until one person mishandles the ball or cannot keep up with the pace. You can expand this drill so one person remains stationary and moves the other person around (only a couple of feet to one side or the other) or both people move each other around working on eyes, feet, and hands. Intersperse this drill a couple of times anywhere in your movement workouts.

Figure 3.17   These two players show how to perform a quick hands drill.

Turn-and-Explode Drill.   This drill positions you at the center of the baseline with your back to the court. The partner should stand at the T (the intersection of the service line and center service line) facing the back of the court (Figure 3.18). The partner should toss a ball gently into the air about 10 to 15 feet high so it lands somewhere in the backcourt area. Just before the ball lands, the partner can give the command of "now." You must turn quickly, find the ball, and explode to catch it before it bounces twice. Obviously, this drill can be made as easy or as hard as you need it to be. Try about 8 to 10 of these in each session.

Z-Ball Coordination Drill.   This drill employs a lop-sided rubber ball called a Z-ball that can be purchased at many toy stores (Figure 3.19).

Figure 3.18   Stand at the baseline with your back to the court. Your partner says "now" just before the ball lands. You then turn, react, and catch the ball before it bounces twice.

Figure 3.19   The Z-ball is a lop-sided rubber ball.

You can be as innovative as you want with the Z-ball. This is one drill: Toss the ball in the air, let it bounce, and try to catch it before it bounces twice (Figure 3.20). We have had much success in training eye-hand-feet coordination with Z-ball drills.

SAMPLE MOVEMENT DRILL WORKOUT*

I.   Warm-up
II. Mild stretching
III. Ball reaction drill—4 times for 10 seconds each with 20 to 25 seconds rest between each

Figure 3.20   The movement path of a Z-ball after a bounce is unpredictable due to its shape. Trying to catch it after a bounce can improve eye-hand-feet coordination.

IV.   Toss-and-catch drill—4 times for 10 seconds each with 20 to 25 seconds rest between each

V.   Roll-and-catch drill—4 times for 10 seconds each with 20 to 25 seconds rest between each; then 90 seconds rest to simulate the changeover between games.

VI.   Toss- or roll-and-catch drill—4 times for 10 seconds each with 20 to 25 seconds rest between each

VII.   Hexagon drill—2 times with 30 seconds rest between each

VIII.   Spider run—1 time with 30 seconds rest

IX.   Alley lunges—2 times, 10 lunges each time, with 20 to 25 seconds rest between each set of 10

X.   Alley hops—2 times, 10 hops each time, with 20 to 25 seconds rest between each set of 10

XI.   Eye-hand coordination drills—8 to 10 times for each hand

XII.   90 seconds rest

XIII.   Partner quick hands drill—1 time

XIV.   Turn-and-explode drill—10 times

XV.   Z-ball drill—10 times

*This is only a sample program. Your personal program should be prescribed by your tennis teaching professional (with these concepts in mind) and should be for healthy, active individuals. In other words, you should be fit before doing drills; don't use these drills to get fit.

NET RESULTS

When working on your movement, the emphasis should be on quality, not quantity. Doing more of the footwork is *not* necessarily better. Do the prescribed amount about twice a week and you should see improvement in your court coverage within a few weeks. Quickness in tennis results as much from awareness of the opponent's shot and of what to do in response as from the actual execution of motion itself. For that reason, focus on the ball and try the three Rs: ready, read, react! Always be ready as the opponent starts to swing, read and immediately react on every shot (even if it's coming right to you), and then explode to the ball. These are the keys to being a better mover on the court.

Control Versus Power— Which Is More Important?

The correct usage of control and power is probably the single most important factor in separating the great players from the good ones. Elite tennis players know how to mix high-speed shots with slower controlled shots. They instinctively know how hard to swing in certain situations to produce the best results. In short, they hit every ball with a purpose, using an optimal combination of force and control.

As a player desiring to improve your competitive ability, what should you strive for? How can you best achieve stroke consistency and mix it with the power necessary to perform at a higher level? The answers to these two questions will be discussed in this chapter. However, the first thing we must do is differentiate between control and power.

Some authorities define control simply as getting the ball in play as often as possible. Others who are a bit more philosophical say that control in tennis is hitting the last ball in the court. Both are adequate definitions, but neither really helps us understand control, because control in a tennis match really depends a lot on the situation at hand. For example, what is control when it's your serve at 4-5 in the third, 30-40, and you find yourself on the run for a wide backhand while the opponent is about 8 feet from the net ready to pounce on anything you hit? Some of you might say, "Lob and keep the ball in play." Others might feel, "Just get it in; at least, make him or her hit a winner to beat me!" And the killers out there might think, "I'll go for it, a screamer down the line!" Control for these players is quite different. The control needed to merely keep the ball in play isn't nearly as difficult as that necessary for the screamer down the line.

Hitting with power doesn't necessarily mean you have to kill the ball to be effective. If you strike a ball with all your might, as a baseball batter might when going for the left field fence, your body parts work to generate the highest racket velocity possible. When you swing only for maximum power, your body parts don't care whether the ball makes it over the net or inside the lines on the other side of the net; they are only trying to provide the ball with as much impetus as possible. In tennis, you must be concerned about controlling the ball's flight so it stays inside the court boundaries yet is penetrating enough to keep the opponent on the defensive. Therefore, hitting with power means that you optimize the action between body parts to hit a high-velocity stroke and still maintain good control. The pros call this being able to get a "good stick on the ball." But remember, it doesn't matter how hard you hit the ball; it still has to land in the court!

Avoid Those Costly Errors

Keeping the ball in play is, of course, vital. Mistakes are killers! And mistakes occur more often than winners. Many of the game's greatest coaches feel that more than 75 percent of all points scored in a match are due to errors. Let's look at one of the closest matches in NCAA history. Table 4.1 examines the 1978 NCAA singles final between John McEnroe and John Sadri and compares the total errors committed and total outright winners made during a 4-set match that McEnroe won: 7-6(5-3), 7-6(5-3), 5-7, 7-6(5-3). Utilizing a 9-point tie-breaker format, this was an extremely close match with only 2 points separating winning from losing: 144 points for McEnroe and 142 for Sadri. Note especially that although Sadri served 21 more aces than McEnroe, he also committed 26 more stroking errors.

Table 4.2 depicts a 1987 match between Steffi Graf and Martina Navratilova. As you can see, time has not changed the fact that most tennis matches are won on errors, not winners. The score of this French Open final was 6-4, 4-6, 8-6 in favor of Graf. The score was close but so were the statistics. Total outright winners were 38-35 in favor of Graf, but unforced errors (the real culprit responsible in losing a match) were 32 for Graf and 39 for Navratilova.

Table 4.1   Match Statistical Summary 94th NCAA Singles Championship*

John McEnroe Versus John Sadri
May 29, 1978
Athens, Georgia

	McEnroe	Sadri
Total errors committed	61	87
Forehand	19	30
Backhand	42	57
Crosscourt	29	37
Straight ahead	32	50
Hit from backcourt	47	63
Hit from midcourt	4	10
Hit from net	10	14
Long	14	21
Wide	14	17
Net	30	48
Long and wide	3	1
Double faults	6	8
Total outright winners	46	51
Forehand	28	35
Backhand	18	16
Crosscourt	23	18
Straight ahead	23	33
Hit from backcourt	14	15
Hit from midcourt	6	13
Hit from net	26	23
Aces	3	24
Percent first serves in	70	56

Match score: McEnroe defeated Sadri 7-6 (5-3), 7-6 (5-3), 5-7, 7-6 (5-3).
Time of match: 4 hr 15 min.

*From Hensley (1979).

Various Game Styles

You obviously need to strive for consistency as a key strategy in your game. But, you can't sacrifice ball speed just to keep the ball in play. Before discussing how you can hit with both velocity and control, let's

Table 4.2   The French Open Championship Match Between Steffi Graf and Martina Navratilova (Courtesy of Computennis)

Item	Graf	Navratilova
Aces	4	2
Service winners	2	1
Double faults	2	6
First-serve percent	80	68
Percent first-serve points won	52	55
Service games held	12	11
Break points against	12	12
Service games broken	5	6
Winners	38	35
Points won forcing	64	67
Unforced errors	32	39
Percent backcourt points won	48	44
Advances to net	21	98
Points won at net	11	58
Total points won	103	99

examine the game styles of different pros. This will show that you can play many different ways and still net excellent results.

The game has seen many different styles of play that were and still are successful. Laver could vary speeds and spins well, Smith dominated with a big serve-and-volley game, and McEnroe came along with the finesse and artistry of a genius. The word on Connors and Agassi would be two speeds—hard and harder—whereas Becker hits serves like BBs out of an air rifle. In the women's game, King and Navratilova will be known as the great serve and volleyers, Evert will always remain the steady and graceful ground stroker, Graf and Capriati combine speed and power, and Sabatini hits the heavy topspin high over the net and deep into the court.

All of these pros use different match strategies because of the ways they hit the ball. Borg was said to have an unorthodox swing with a severe racket roll during the follow-through. McEnroe seems to stand straight up as he swings, and Agassi looks as though he actually tries to jump off the ground as he tries to hit every forehand as hard as possible. The unique part of each style is that the basic laws of physics govern what each player does to hit the ball so well. These principles of physics will assist you in learning to hit with optimal control and power.

Four Goals
for Every Player of Any Skill Level

No matter what the skill level of the player I'm working with, I want that player to strive for four goals. These goals are, in order,

1. control,
2. consistency,
3. depth, and
4. power.

All are related to one another but each must be developed and understood independently. For example, each player must first learn control of the ball as well as control of his or her body. Remember, no matter how hard you hit the ball, it has to stay in the court. Second, a player needs to develop consistency of movements so shot consistency will be developed as well.

Once you have control and consistency, you can learn how to hit with depth into the court by using more net clearance on your shots. Consistently deep, penetrating shots on your part will spell the downfall for most of your opponents. You could learn to hit with depth as you learn control and consistency, but I don't want you dealing with too many things as you learn to be a better player. Controlling the ball and making your shots consistent with proper technique are crucial prerequisites for adding depth to your competitive repertoire. Finally, power can be brought into your game style. Again, it's true that you could learn to hit with power as you develop control, consistency, and depth, but this approach of one thing at a time works! Don't try to do too much, too fast, too soon. It could make the game very frustrating.

Dr. Jack's Tennis Tips

When working on control, swing the hands slowly with accuracy. You must develop speed with your legs, hips, and trunk, but you should never think of swinging hard with your hand. The slow hand movements will also help you develop consistency later on. When you begin hitting with depth, don't try to hit harder; simply hit the ball higher over the net! Depth into the court does not necessarily connote velocity. Gradually, increase the speed of your shot to develop power, but try to not sacrifice control, consistency, or depth!

The Body's Sources of Power:
Linear and Angular Momentum

Two very simple concepts affect hitting a ball with control and high velocity, and both involve a transfer of momentum: linear momentum and angular momentum (Figure 4.1). These two sources of power should act together in a coordinated manner. In chapter 1 I discussed how the trans-

a　　　　　　　　　　　b

c　　　　　　　　　　　d

Figure 4.1　Notice how this athlete transfers linear momentum forward by stepping into the shot (a and b). The angular momentum is then generated by body rotation (c and d).

fer of linear and angular momentum is accomplished: by stepping into the shot and rotating the upper body, respectively.

Momentum and the Backswing

The upper body rotation is similar for both closed- and open-stance strokes and is initiated at the backswing. One of the biggest controversies among tennis players and their coaches is which backswing—straight back, small loop, or large loop—provides the best racket velocity and control. The traditional train of thought was that a straight-back preparation (Figure 4.2) allowed the most control, whereas the large-loop backswing (Figure 4.3), allowed the highest racket velocity. Sport scientists tell us it's true that high racket velocity is generated by the large-loop backswing, but control can be a real problem with that backswing because of the timing necessary to hit a ball effectively. Research has found that the small-loop backswing (Figure 4.4) not only allows for an excellent combination of velocity and control but, just as importantly, helps the body maintain its rhythm during each stroke. This helps the athlete stabilize timing in hitting a ball and avoid the timing problems caused by the large-loop backswing. When you're establishing a stroking rhythm, the small-loop preparation also facilitates the generation of linear and angular momentum by initiating the trunk rotation.

a   b   c

Figure 4.2 This player shows how a forehand drive is hit with a straight-back backswing.

Figure 4.3 This player demonstrates how to use a large-loop backswing to hit a forehand drive. Note the height of the hand.

Figure 4.4 In this sequence you can see how a forehand should be hit with a small-loop backswing. Note the height of the hand.

Momentum and Footwork

Because the body rotation is more pronounced for an open-stance stroke, we will use this as an example of how the transfer of angular momentum occurs before we consider the role of momentum in a forward-step stroke.

Footwork in Open-Stance Ground Stroke

First we need to discuss the footwork involved in effectively hitting a stroke with an open stance. There is obviously little transfer of linear momentum forward into the stroke because the motion of the foot closest to the ball is either directly to the side or slightly behind the impact point (only in a few cases is the side step forward). There's a specific reason for the side step, however. As you can see in Figure 4.5, the side step allows the hips and trunk to rotate backward during the backswing. Just prior to the forward swing, there will be a slight push-off by the foot closest to the ball. This force, exerted by the ground, passes through the leg and follows a specific course of action, as depicted by Figure 4.6. After traveling up the legs, it is received by the hips, which begin accelerating in a rotary fashion. When the hips reach a certain optimal angular velocity (the word *optimal* is used here instead of *maximal* because tennis usually doesn't require maximum force), the trunk reaches its optimal angular velocity, and the upper limb begins to move about the shoulder. The sum of all these integrated forces then results in optimal acceleration of the racket. When coordinated correctly, this transfer of angular momentum is the factor that can make an open-stance ground stroke so effective.

a   b

Figure 4.5 This individual demonstrates how the unit turn is employed in his efficient open-stance forehand drive.

STROKE SEQUENCE:

GROUND REACTION FORCE
↓
LEGS
↓
HIPS
↓
TRUNK
↓
UPPER LIMB
↓
RACQUET

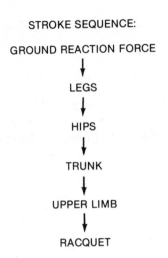

Figure 4.6   This is the sequence of events that occurs as force is transferred.

Jimmy Connors can serve as an excellent example of someone who has always used little linear momentum but who maximized his angular momentum. The mechanics of Connors's forehand can be viewed in Figure 4.7. You can easily see how the body's rotation brings the racket head toward impact so well. However, notice when Jimmy leaves the ground during his forehand. In his famous jumping forehand he doesn't leave the ground until just before impact. Therefore, when you see

a   b

Figure 4.7   Notice how Jimmy Connors utilizes no step forward in this forehand drive but how he maximizes his body rotation.

Connors a foot and a half off the ground during his strokes, you should remember that he doesn't leave the ground until the very last instant. If Connors jumped any sooner than that, he would lose a great deal of the angular momentum he had generated. In other words, if he left the ground before all the generated force had reached his smaller body parts (the forearm and hand), Newton's third law (action-reaction) dictates that his larger body parts would react and not send the force forward to the upper limb. Thus, the key to Connors's great open-stance forehand is timing.

Footwork in the Forward-Step Stroke

Although the open-stance ground stroke can be utilized to hit very effective shots, it isn't that easy to perform, which is why the traditional step into the ball is more often recommended. This seems reasonable because this conventional approach permits players to have better control over their bodies, usually allowing the stroke to be more efficient. However, this approach still necessitates synchronizing linear and angular momentum. The timing of the step forward and its coordination with the system of chain links are significant. Many books say to step forward into the shot and swing. It's not that easy!

As the player in Figure 4.8 faces the net and readies to swing forward for a forehand drive, the foot opposite the forehand side of the body

a   b

Figure 4.8 This player demonstrates how to hit a forehand drive by using the proper stepping action. Notice how the front foot is placed forward and slightly to the side.

steps across and forward in a normal stridelike fashion. The foot is placed directly toward the point of ball contact or directly forward toward the net. While the opposite foot strides forward, there is an obvious push-off from the hind foot to initiate weight transfer. Once the front foot is planted and supports a large proportion of body weight, the transfer of linear momentum is complete. At this point, the force generated from the push-off reaches the hips, which begin rotating. This is the important transition: the initiation of angular momentum, through hip rotation, from the linear push-off of the hind leg. The trunk begins its involvement by rotating very soon after the hip rotation begins. The upper arm then quickly brings the racket forward toward impact.

Therefore, the transition between linear momentum and angular momentum is crucial. A mistake in timing could severely hamper stroke production. To help my students understand this timing, I offer a simple phrase for them to think about when practicing: Step, then swing. I also tell them to attempt to make their strokes as rhythmic as possible. The rhythm, once learned, will allow the student to graduate to more advanced strokes (e.g., hitting a high ground stroke with topspin). This same rhythmic swing enables players to hit incredibly hard shots with seemingly effortless movement and thus to hit what's known as a solid ball.

The Solid (or Heavy) Ball

I'll never forget the first time I hit against Tim Gullikson (1991 Wimbledon 35-and-over singles champion). I was really pumped up by getting to work out with such a great player. The shots I hit were the best I could muster, but there was one problem that quickly became apparent. I was hitting my best shots, but Tim was returning every ball harder than I had hit the previous stroke. Oddly enough, he didn't seem to swing the racket very fast at all, but he still hit an incredibly solid ball.

The solid, or heavy, ball is a widely misunderstood concept that is most often used at the advanced levels of tennis. Two types of tennis shots exist that are classified as solid balls: a stroke with a great deal of velocity that feels like it will knock the racket out of your hand, and a hard ground stroke hit with extreme topspin that seems to take away control of your own shot. How do players develop these awesome strokes?

Hitting a solid ball is one of the key elements in developing offensive ground strokes and service returns. The implications of this are extremely important. By learning to hit a solid ball, you can develop an aggressive, attacking game without having to depend exclusively on the serve-and-volley style of play.

The ability to hit a solid ball depends on how well you can execute the following seven factors.

- Using all body parts sufficiently and in synchrony
- Contacting the ball in the hitting zone of the racket face
- Using a firm grip to enhance control and to help with transferring force to the ball
- Meeting the ball with the wrist (or wrists, if hitting a two-handed shot) and elbow (or elbows) firm
- Imparting the proper amount of spin on the ball
- Hitting the ball with a complete follow-through
- Contacting the ball in your strike zone

Using All Body Parts Sufficiently and in Synchrony

You are already aware of the importance of the body's linked system, but there is a very fundamental way of understanding why you may not be hitting the ball as well as you want. To review, virtually all tennis strokes involve force created against the ground and transferred up through the legs, hips, trunk, and arms. Not only is this successive summation of forces integral to successful performance in tennis, but there is also a continuity by which it must be achieved. In other words, the timing is crucial. For example, once the legs reach their peak velocity, that velocity is transferred to the hips. When the hips reach their peak rotational velocity, the velocity in the body's linked system, that velocity is transferred to the trunk, and so on (Figure 4.9). A problem becomes

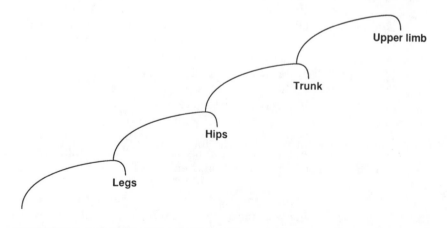

Figure 4.9   This represents an efficient force transfer from the legs to the upper limb.

apparent when movement is inefficient, which not only can cause an error in stroke production but also creates the potential for injury.

One aspect of an inefficient action of the linked system occurs when a body part is left out of the movement. This means that a subsequent body segment must work harder if the same result is to be achieved. For example, imagine a two-handed backhand hit with no trunk rotation. The arms must swing the racket very hard, using more muscular effort than normal to generate a proper racket head speed.

A second form of inefficient stroke production occurs when all the body parts are used but not employed correctly. For example, a player, when hitting a serve, may utilize the hips but may block them from rotating properly. This will require the trunk and upper limb to work much harder to generate the correct amount of racket head speed.

The final form of stroke inefficiency takes place when the body parts in the linked system are not properly synchronized. This is the timing on which so many tennis players blame their mistakes. For example, a player may have a hitch in his or her service motion. When this hitch occurs, it throws the complete timing mechanism of the body's linked system out of synchrony. The arm then has to make up for this lack of proper timing by forcefully swinging the racket forward with excessive muscular action.

Contacting the Ball in the Hitting Zone of the Racket Face

It's very interesting to me how many people use the term *sweet spot* to describe the spot on the racket face where they feel the ball should be hit. Technically speaking, the sweet spot is the center of percussion of the racket and is usually located somewhere between the center of the strings and the throat of the racket itself. Contrary to what many believe, the sweet spot is a very tiny point on the racket face. It's virtually impossible to hit a ball in the sweet spot all the time. However, there is a small area surrounding the sweet spot with which effective shots can be hit (Figure 4.10). It seems more appropriate to speak of contacting a ball in this hitting zone of the racket face. The hitting zone is an area ranging anywhere from 2 to 4 inches wide (depending on the size of the racket head) surrounding the sweet spot. Contacting the ball in the hitting zone results in little racket head rotation and enhances the control of your shot.

It's difficult to practice contacting the ball in the hitting zone of the racket. When you swing your racket forward toward the ball, it's almost impossible to gauge exactly where impact will occur. Even the pros occasionally hit balls off the frames of their rackets. If you feel a lot of racket rotation in your hand at ball contact, you can work on two things. First,

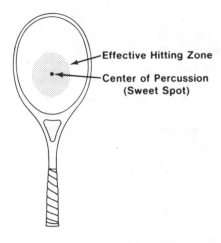

Figure 4.10 The darkened area on the racket face indicates the size of the racket's hitting zone.

try to slow down your forward swing and simply concentrate on making a firm impact with the ball. Although you have no control over the velocity of the oncoming ball, you can improve your accuracy by slowing the hands and using the larger body parts to create racket speed. The second thing you can work on is your grip firmness.

Dr. Jack's Tennis Tips

For some players, slowing down the racket head will work very well. However, if you are a good player (5.0 on the National Tennis Rating Program [NTRP] or above) or if you are nervous in a match, you might have to swing a little faster to maintain a sense of rhythm. Just remember to drive the ball with your legs, hips, and trunk, not your hand. Regardless of what you do, think of hitting the ball as "sweetly" as you can every time.

Using a Firm Grip to Enhance Control and Transfer Force to the Ball

Numerous biomechanical and tennis authorities believe that grip firmness is an important, sometimes the most important, factor in hitting a tennis ball well. By maintaining a firm grip, the player reduces racket recoil and thereby increases the force applied to the ball. However, a controversy has erupted concerning the degree of grip firmness a player should maintain during a stroke. The cause of this debate stems from the research on grip firmness conducted in the late 1970s and throughout the 1980s. Several scientists studied the rebound of a tennis ball as it was fired against the center of a racket under two conditions: the racket firmly clamped in a vise grip, and the racket standing balanced on its butt end. In other words, the researchers simulated two extremes of grip firmness: a very strong grip and no grip at all. Amazingly, the ball rebounded with similar velocities in both cases. Researchers concluded that there is no time for the racket to move appreciably while impact occurs, so the effect of a free-standing racket on ball speed equaled that of a clamped racket. This implies that grip firmness may not be that important. Bear in mind, however, that these studies were concerned with central impacts on a motionless racket; we already know that a large majority of impacts are off center.

My colleagues and I conducted an experiment to determine the effects of grip firmness for off-center ball contacts. Balls were impacted against a racket when it was free to rotate and when it was firmly clamped at the handle. We found that ball rebound velocities were slightly (although not significantly) higher in the clamped situation for respective off-center contacts. The important observation, however, was that with the clamped condition each ball rebounded directly out from the racket face. For the free-to-rotate condition, the ball left the racket at an errant angle. Therefore, it seemed that regardless of the effect of grip firmness on rebound velocity, the lack of a firm grip causes poor ball control.

Bruce Elliott has done some of the more contemporary work in this area. Instead of using motionless rackets, he constructed a mechanical arm with a hand grasp that would hold the racket with varying firmness. As a ball was fired from a ball machine, the racket arm was triggered and swung forward with velocity comparable to that of a skilled male player. Elliott found a 7 percent reduction in rebound velocities from the firm to the light grip. He concluded that a firm grip was absolutely necessary to increase the power of a stroke and to improve control. We know today that this still holds true and, in fact, is magnified if you use a wide body racket.

We know that a firm grip is required in tennis, so let's discuss what makes a firm grip. If you simply hold the racket in front of you, your grip is probably very light, just tight enough to support the racket. If you swing at a ball with this grip, two things will probably happen: The racket will fly out of your hand as it is swung forward, and the muscles of your forearm will not be set to control the racket during impact and you'll lose control of the shot. When preparing to hit a shot you can maintain a light grip during the backswing, but as you swing the racket forward you should squeeze the grip firmly to enhance your stroke. The grip need not be a death grip, but it should be firm enough to minimize racket rotation at impact.

For a racket to have sufficient impetus when hitting a shot, force must be generated from other body parts. The transfer of force through these body segments culminates with the hand giving impetus to the racket. Therefore, a firm grip is of utmost importance because it serves as the final link in this transfer of momentum.

There is a point of no return as far as grip firmness goes, however. Newton's third law says that for every action, there's an equal and opposite reaction. The tighter you squeeze the racket, the more force that's transmitted to your hand and forearm, especially from those off-center impacts. It will take practice to determine how firm your grip should be. If the racket turns in your hand or if you have difficulty with control, your grip may be too loose. If you experience a great deal of vibration or force into your hand, forearm, and elbow, loosen your grip a bit and refer to the section in chapter 2 on grip selection to be sure you're using the correct grip size.

It seems to me that the controversy concerning grip firmness should be put to rest. When awaiting the opponent's shot, you should use a loose grip. However, I must recommend a firm grip at impact for several reasons:

- To maintain control over the racket head as it readies to hit the ball
- To provide optimal racket velocity as it's swung forward
- To impart ample force to the ball at impact
- To prevent the racket from twisting in your hand during ball contact
- To effectively link the force generated by the body's kinetic chain to the racket

Meeting the Ball
With the Wrists and Elbows Completely Firm

Keeping the wrist (or wrists) firm when meeting the ball is another integral part of hitting a solid ball, as is keeping the elbow (or elbows) firm. It is possible to hit a fairly hard shot by spinning the ball with a large vertical swing, but the shot won't be nearly as heavy as if the ball is driven deep with optimal spin. Here's why!

As force is transferred through the body's kinetic chain, it must pass from the trunk to the upper limb. The three joints in the upper limb (shoulder, elbow, and wrist) are integral in ensuring that optimal force reaches the racket. When a player attempts to hit a solid ball, there should be no excessive wrist or elbow movement regardless of the shot type attempted.

Remember that there are two ways to hit a solid ball: by hitting a high-velocity shot and by hitting a hard shot with heavy topspin or underspin. Wrist and elbow firmness is necessary in both situations. When you hit a hard stroke, the upper limb joints need to maximize the force transfer from the trunk. When you want to hit a solid ball with a great deal of spin, you still should not use excessive joint action.

Although spin production is discussed in depth in chapter 6, there are some things you should be aware of relative to this topic. For example, you can incorporate the wrist and elbow to hit a lot of topspin on the ball but not to hit a high-velocity shot with heavy topspin. Borg can serve as an example of someone who hit fairly hard and with much topspin. Many people felt he was a wristy player because of his exaggerated follow-through. However, a high-speed film analysis, represented in Figure 4.11, shows that Borg's elbow and wrist moved very little before impact but moved a great deal after the ball was hit. It was the controlled, vertical racket head action that allowed him to hit a heavy ball with topspin.

Figure 4.11   Observe how little upper limb joint action occurs during this athlete's topspin forehand drive.

Imparting the Proper Amount of Spin on the Ball

The correct amount of spin simply means enough spin to keep the ball from going out and to keep the opponent on the defensive (see chapter 6). Too much spin takes away from the horizontal velocity of the ball, because spin is caused by the vertical motion of the racket. When the racket moves vertically to produce spin, you sacrifice forward racket speed. Figure 4.12a shows the racket motion when a ball is hit with little topspin. In contrast, Figure 4.12b depicts the racket motion during a

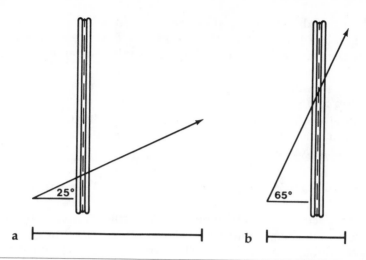

Figure 4.12   These diagrams depict the linear racket motion during (a) slight topspin and (b) heavy topspin.

heavy topspin stroke. Figure 4.13a and b illustrates strokes in which the ball is hit with slight underspin and heavy underspin. In all four cases, the racket travels the same total distance (as denoted by the length of the arrows), but the forward motion is shortened when the racket imparts excessive topspin or underspin. When the forward motion is less and still occurs over the same time period, the ball will not receive as much

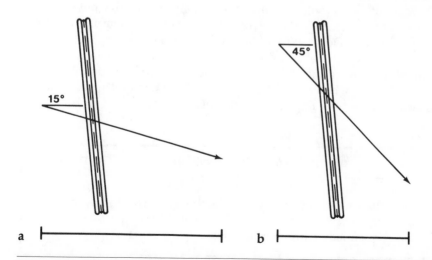

Figure 4.13   These pictures illustrate the racket movement necessary to hit (a) slight underspin and (b) heavy underspin.

forward force and will not travel as fast. A common mistake of many advanced players is using excessive spins and still trying to hit the ball very hard. Very few players can hit a lot of spin and consistently maintain control.

You should work on hitting shots that clear the net by 4 to 6 feet and go deep into your opponent's court. To do this you'll have to hit penetrating strokes with slight spin. Having depth in the court and clearance above the net as your practice goals, you should see significant improvement in your shots.

Hitting the Ball With a Complete Follow-Through

Some of the factors that determine how well you hit a solid ball are difficult to monitor (e.g., where the ball hits on the racket face). However, follow-through may be the most important factor over which you have total control. The only way you can hit penetrating ground strokes is to swing the racket head through impact effectively. Until the ball is hit, there cannot be racket head deceleration during the forward swing. Even though the ball is already hit, you can learn a great deal about your stroke from how you follow through.

Many players finish their follow-throughs with their rackets pointing high, across the net, or both (Figure 4.14). This means that their swings must follow an arc while traveling from the fully prepared position to the end of the follow-through. Other players wrap their rackets over their shoulders, as you see in Figure 4.15. And still others follow through with their racket faces directed skyward, as demonstrated in Figure 4.16. There is nothing wrong with any of these follow-throughs, but you must consider one thing as you accelerate the racket through impact into your follow-through. Don't think of how you will follow through but of how the racket face will travel through impact. One cue I give my athletes is to think of making the strings follow the ball as long as possible when it's hit. Players who remember that phrase have had pretty good success in swinging through impact with control.

Dr. Jack's Tennis Tips

To ensure a good impact, try to make the racket face follow the ball. Another way to look at this is to think of hitting three imaginary balls sequentially with your one stroke.

Figure 4.14   These photos show the athlete's follow-through ending with the racket pointing high.

A complete swing with a full follow-through is necessary to achieve maximum velocity while imparting the correct amount of spin on the ball. In order to hit through the ball, you must strive to hit it well in front of your body midline (Figure 4.17). Hitting the ball behind the middle of the body forces you to swing upward quickly and thus not hit the ball

Figure 4.15 This is a wrap follow-through for a two-handed backhand.

Figure 4.16 This athlete demonstrates a follow-through in which the racket faces skyward.

effectively (Figure 4.18). A forward contact point will allow you to transfer all bodily forces to the upper limb and to attain a high racket velocity. As you hit the ball, practice a long follow-through after impact. This will help you to continue accelerating the racket through impact. If the follow-through is abbreviated, it's a sure bet that you started slowing down the racket before you hit the ball.

Figure 4.17   Notice where ball contact will occur for these athletes.

Figure 4.18   When you are forced to hit the ball behind your body midline, your swing will usually be abrupt with little direct force behind it.

Contacting the Ball in Your Strike Zone

The final component of hitting a solid ball is meeting the ball at the optimum height for your body. This is a big factor in separating good tournament players from pros. Most competitors often let the ball get too low before hitting it, which makes a penetrating ground stroke difficult to hit. With one extra step or step-and-a-half forward, aggressive ground strokes are within reach. Figure 4.19 illustrates three different heights at which a ball may be met.

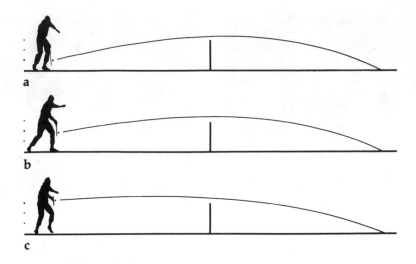

Figure 4.19 These diagrams illustrate how much easier it is to hit a penetrating ground stroke when you strive for a proper impact point relative to your body. Observe the different points of ball contact: (a) near ankle level, (b) slightly above knee level, and (c) near waist height. Also note the respective ball flight trajectories from those impact points. Therefore, you should strive to contact a ball near waist height whenever possible.

Figure 4.19a shows a ball that has been hit about 12 inches above the ground (well below knee level for someone 6 feet tall). The ball must follow a fairly steep upward path to clear the net and land deep in the opponent's court. If you wish to swing hard at the ball, you have to impart a lot of topspin on the ball so it will land within the court boundaries. Although heavy topspin is one way to hit a solid ball, I think you'll see how much easier it is if the contact point is a little higher above the ground.

The ball in Figure 4.19b is met just below net level (2-1/2 feet high). Any high-velocity shot must follow a slightly upward path so gravity won't pull the ball into the net. The amount of spin necessary to bring the ball into the court is less than that required in Figure 4.19a (assuming the two balls are hit at the same velocity). Because the ball in Figure 4.19b doesn't have to be hit with as much upward trajectory as the one in Figure 4.19a, the stroke could provide higher ball velocity even though the ball still might have too much topspin to give the true effect of a solid ball.

The ball in Figure 4.19c is at the ideal height for a 6-foot-tall person to hit a solid ball: approximately waist height or slightly above. The ball does not have to follow a steep upward path to land with depth in the opponent's backcourt and requires less spin to keep it within the court boundaries. The ball in Figure 4.19c can travel at a higher rate of speed, making it a more offensive shot.

Dr. Jack's Tennis Tips

There is basically one way to position your body so the ball is contacted in your strike zone. As you prepare to hit each stroke, you must move your feet. By quickly moving forward on a short low-bouncing ball, hitting a ball on the rise, or moving backward on a deep, high-bouncing ball, you'll be amazed at how your strokes will improve. As well as enabling you to hit a consistently solid ball, this technique will allow your stroke to move in a similar pattern each time, making all of your shots more consistent.

NET RESULTS

As you practice generating more force behind your shots, always be aware that tennis is basically a control game. Power will do little good if you have no control over your shots. Slowly try to combine the benefits of your body's physical capabilities by utilizing linear and angular momentum in an optimum combination. By using your body parts in synchrony, you will develop a sound power supply. Don't try to hit excessive spins, but think of driving the ball deep into your opponent's court. Proper footwork will also help you reach your goal of hitting a solid ball. By hitting the ball at the desirable height relative to the court and to your body, you will be able to optimize your force transfer to the ball.

Therefore, try to pay careful attention to the concepts described in this chapter. If you practice them diligently, you should be able to greatly improve your ground strokes. By learning to hit consistently aggressive ground strokes, you will be capable of playing an offensive, attacking game without having to rely on the serve-and-volley style of play. Due to tremendous changes that tennis has undergone in the past few years (e.g., slower courts and high-performance rackets), hitting offensive ground strokes is quickly becoming the way to develop a winning tennis game. Development of these types of ground strokes combined with shot consistency should be the goal of every tournament player.

C H A P T E R 5

The One-Handed Versus the Two-Handed Backhand: Which Is Better?

Ｈow would you react if I told you that a two-handed backhand is easier to hit than a one-handed backhand? What if you read that there is very little difference in reach between one-handed and two-handed backhands? I feel that both of these statements are true, and though many traditionalists might argue vehemently against them, these arguments are outdated when compared to the findings of recent sport science research. Before applying the results of this research to your game, we should discuss how these strokes came into being and how various authorities view them.

The one-handed backhand has been used since tennis began in the 1870s. The two-handed backhand was virtually unheard of until the 1930s, when Vivian McGrath became the world's first highly ranked player to compete using this stroke. Very few players used the two-handed backhand after that until the 1970s, when the stroke became popular because of Bjorn Borg, Chris Evert, Jimmy Connors, and Tracy Austin. But why the sudden return of the two-hander?

What the Experts Say

Authorities offer various reasons for the prominence of the two-handed backhand. Some say today's players used it when they were young because they didn't have enough strength or confidence to control the racket with a one-handed backhand. In Figure 5.1, you can see an excel-

a   b

Figure 5.1   It seems obvious that with two hands on the racket (a), the athlete can better control its motion than when using only one hand (b).

lent tennis player who has a good two-handed backhand but can't hit a one-handed stroke very well. Proponents of the one-handed backhand feel that the two-handed stroke is an affectation and state that the swinging of a tennis racket with both hands is unorthodox and cumbersome. They go on to note that newcomers to the game appear to be caught in the grip of a revolution because of a desire to imitate the top players in the world.

Advocates of both types of backhand drives have proposed that their preferred strokes should be hit similar to a forehand. I believe this is the case with the two-handed backhand but not with the one-handed stroke. In the forehand, for instance, an eastern, semiwestern, or western forehand grip is usually recommended, and ball contact should occur over the front foot. To hit a one-handed backhand effectively, however, a grip change is necessary (from any of the previously noted forehand grips), the ball contact must occur ahead of the front foot (Figure 5.2). In addition, a completely different set of muscles is used for racket control, making similarity of swing mechanics virtually nonexistent. The forehand and two-handed backhand are much more similar, as shown by the contact point in Figure 5.3. To hit a two-handed backhand, two eastern forehand grips can be used (although the base hand can be changed to a continental grip if desired) and ball contact usually occurs over the front foot just as in the forehand. In fact, many say that using a two-handed backhand is just like hitting a forehand from the opposite side.

Figure 5.2   This player demonstrates where ball contact must occur for an effective one-handed backhand drive.

a   b

Figure 5.3   You can see that this player will hit the ball in front of his body with a two-handed-backhand (a), much as he would on a forehand (b).

Reach

Because both hands are used on the two-hander, proponents of the one-handed backhand have time and time again denounced it for its lack of

---

Dr. Jack's Tennis Tips

If you use a two-handed backhand, I recommend you use a continental grip on the base hand (the hand closest to your body). This will alleviate any stress to the arm and allow you more freedom in stroke production.

---

reach. In a high-speed film study I conducted on 36 highly skilled players, I could find no differences in reach between the two strokes when the players were properly prepared to swing. When the players in my study didn't have to run for shot preparation, ball contact for each stroke occurred about the same distance from the body. This statement usually stimulates the following question: What about the situation in which a player is really stretched out for a backhand return? We can visualize how the pros can lunge at a shot with a one-handed backhand, but what about those players utilizing a two-handed backhand? Could they also reach the wide shot? Probably not! However, how many of those lunging one-handed backhands have you seen hit for winners? Very few, I'm sure. Most of those wide shots are returned as defensive underspin drives or lobs; they are not penetrating, offensive strokes. My point is that a player who has an effective two-handed backhand (Figure 5.4) can learn to hit those one-handed lunges and develop a

a   b

Figure 5.4 Although the competitor seen in these figures has an extremely effective two-handed backhand (a), he is quite capable of performing a one-handed lunging maneuver when he is pulled wide of the court (b).

sound defensive underspin drive or lob. Therefore, there is really no rationale for avoiding a two-handed backhand due to a supposed lack of reach, especially on balls you can easily prepare for.

Low-Bouncing Balls

The one shot that could cause a two-hander problems is a low ball in front of the body (Figure 5.5). Obviously, with both hands on the racket,

Figure 5.5   A player using a two-handed backhand often has problems with a low-bouncing ball. The player in this figure has used extremely good footwork to get in position for the return.

the player must get lower to return such a shot offensively. With a one-handed backhand, the body doesn't have to get quite as low to hit the ball effectively. Therefore, the player with a two-handed backhand must get to the ball quicker for a higher ball-contact point or must learn to hit that low shot with one hand, as has the player in Figure 5.6.

Dr. Jack's Tennis Tips

If you are a tournament player or wish to become one, I suggest that you learn a one-handed backhand approach shot. A low shot in front of the body is a major limiting factor for a two-handed backhand. Refer to chapter 9 to study how the approach shot should be hit.

a

b

c

Figure 5.6 Here you see how a player with a two-handed backhand hits an approach shot.

The Role of Muscular Strength

It has been fairly well accepted that the one-handed backhand requires greater strength of the performer. Because only one upper limb is used to generate force in swinging the racket, and because the arm can't rely on trunk action as much as with a two-handed backhand, it makes sense that the one-handed stroke demands more strength. A beginner using a one-handed backhand often cramps the elbow, holding it very close to the body (Figure 5.7), for exactly that reason; the beginner doesn't have the physical capabilities to wield the racket efficiently. In contrast, the cramping motion is not usually seen in the two-handed backhand because the swinging motion necessitates the elbows being fairly close to the body. In addition, the racket should actually be less difficult to swing with two hands around the handle than when only one hand is used.

Figure 5.7 This player really doesn't have the physical capabilities to support and swing the racket with a one-handed backhand. Notice how she is swinging by holding her upper arm close to the body, indicating she needs to support the racket motion with her trunk.

If you have difficulty in swinging the racket with one hand, poor racket head control can result, causing

- poor shot placement,
- difficulty in imparting spin,
- severe turning of the racket head during and after impact, and
- a late ball-contact point.

To prevent these problems, you could lead with the elbow or drop the racket head just prior to impact (Figure 5.8) to help propel the ball over the net.

Using the two-handed backhand could eliminate these difficulties (although not always). It's definitely true that with two hands on the racket handle you can swing upward more effectively and maintain better racket head control, especially when beginning to hit topspin drives.

Spin Production

Strength also plays a significant role in producing topspin. As seen in Figure 5.9, topspin is often difficult to hit using a one-handed backhand due to the additional strength needed to swing the racket at a steep upward angle. In comparison, imparting topspin with a two-handed backhand is simple; strength gained from the use of two hands allows the player to achieve the upward swing angle needed to produce topspin. However, players often have problems maneuvering their rackets in a high-to-low motion for underspin and a side-to-side motion for sidespin. Some two-handers will compensate when hitting an underspin shot by following through with only one hand to facilitate the high-to-

Figure 5.8   Here are two of the movements players often go through in trying to hit a backhand drive over the net: (a) leading with the elbow when preparing to hit the ball and (b) using a great deal of wrist action in trying to make contact with the ball.

Figure 5.9   By comparing (a) and (b), you can see how much more difficult it is to swing the racket with one limb when trying to hit topspin drive.

low action. Notice the athlete in Figure 5.10 as he hits an underspin shot on the backhand side. Although some players follow through with both hands on the racket, many players will follow through with only one hand on the racket. A one-handed follow-through might allow a smoother racket action through impact, facilitating the high-to-low motion for hitting underspin. (Please refer to chapter 6 for specifics about how spin is produced.)

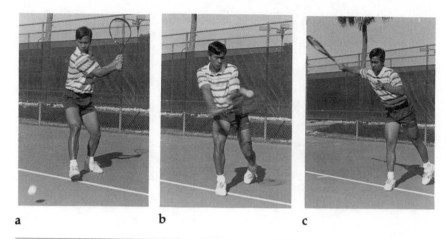

a   b   c

Figure 5.10 This is how a player with a two-handed backhand can hit an underspin backhand and follow through with one hand.

High-Bouncing Balls

Advocates of both backhands have reported that high-bouncing balls can be hit more effectively with their preferred stroke. This all depends on the physical capability of the player and the type of shot to be hit. It's extremely difficult to hit a one-handed backhand with topspin on a ball bouncing at head height. Underspin is usually recommended for this shot, and the ball usually cannot be hit with a very high velocity. In comparison, a player with a two-handed backhand can aggressively hit a head-height ball either flat or with topspin and usually with a higher ball velocity than is possible with one hand (Figure 5.11). It is very difficult to hit a high one-handed backhand flat or with topspin. That's why it's usually recommended that you hit the one-hander with underspin.

Disguise

The two-handed backhand has been lauded for enabling players to disguise shots. It's said that the second hand on the racket can maneuver the racket head at the last possible instant, directing the ball to a part of the court unsuspected by the opponent. If you've ever played a tournament match against someone with a good two-handed backhand, you know such a player can flick his or her wrist at the last second (Figure 5.12) to pass you crosscourt when you are expecting a down-the-line shot. However, the same can be said for a strong player with a good one-handed backhand. The next time you practice with someone who

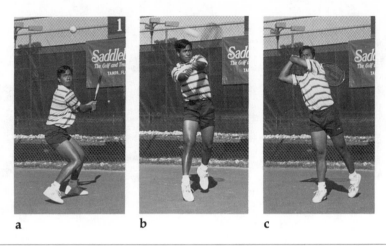

a   b   c

Figure 5.11   This player demonstrates how to hit a high two-handed back-hand.

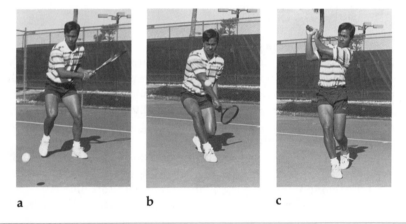

a   b   c

Figure 5.12   The two-handed backhand easily allows you to disguise shots, be-cause the hands can easily change the direction of the racket face.

has an excellent one-handed backhand, stand at the net and practice a volley-passing shot drill. After you've hit a couple of volleys in the drill, your opponent should try to pass you either down the line or crosscourt. Your job is to read the passing shot before it is hit. If your opponent is skilled at this type of drill, I think you'll find that a good one-handed backhand can also be well disguised (Figure 5.13).

a   b

Figure 5.13 This athlete demonstrates that a similar wrist flick may be seen when hitting a short crosscourt one-handed backhand.

With all this information in mind, what decisions can we make about the two types of backhand drives? Both strokes have some obvious advantages and disadvantages, noted earlier in this chapter. Also, some of the claims made for or against one of the strokes may be unjustified. This information can help you determine how your backhand might be enhanced by using either technique, but we can go a step further into our analysis. By studying the two strokes from a sport scientist's viewpoint, you'll get the answers to some of your unresolved questions.

What Sport Science Tells Us

Do you remember the high-speed film study discussed earlier, in which the backhand techniques of 36 highly skilled tennis players (18 for each stroke) were analyzed? For a trial to be successful, the ball had to follow a similar trajectory, regardless of stroke type. This meant that the rackets of all players had to be doing the same thing at impact, again regardless of stroke type. One significant finding dealt with the number of body parts used in each stroke and how they're properly coordinated. For example, all players using each stroke type had a small circular backswing. This enabled each person to have a slightly higher racket head speed at impact than with a straight-back backswing and thus to hit a high-velocity shot.

Dr. Jack's Tennis Tips

As you prepare to hit a backhand, one-handed or two-handed, pretend your name is written on your back and rotate your trunk enough so your opponent can read your name.

For the one-handed backhand, researchers found that five distinct body parts are used prior to impact. After the player in Figure 5.14 steps toward the ball the hips turn slightly, transferring momentum to the trunk, which begins rotating. Then the upper arm moves about the shoulder. This upper arm motion is transferred to slight forearm movement, which in turn causes the hand and racket to position for ball contact. Ball contact must occur about 12 to 14 inches ahead of the front foot to ensure transfer of momentum along all these body parts and to orient the racket face vertically with respect to ball flight.

a   b   c

Figure 5.14   You can see how the different body parts are used when hitting a one-handed backhand drive. Notice that there is slight hip and trunk rotation during the swing and that the hip and trunk do not completely open up until the ball has been hit.

Dr. Jack's Tennis Tips

When you follow through on the one-handed backhand, have your knuckles follow the ball off the racket and then face the sky.

It's coordinating those five body parts that causes many people to have trouble playing tennis with a one-handed backhand. How many times have you seen a player lead with the elbow or drop the racket head to help hit the ball over the net? Such a player is able to use the major body parts, but when it comes to transferring the momentum to the forearm through the elbow, this player loses the coordinated pattern and leads with the elbow. Or a player may be able to transfer the momentum through the elbow to the forearm well but can't get it by the wrist efficiently and severely drops the racket head, causing an awkward follow-through. The two-handed backhand is a different story.

Dr. Jack's Tennis Tips

I feel the main point of a one-handed backhand is the front shoulder (the right shoulder for a right-handed player). Pretend there is a line between your two shoulders; as your shoulders fire around toward impact, try to fix the front shoulder so it's pointing toward where the ball will be hit and then accelerate the racket arm toward impact.

The two-handed stroke only utilizes two body parts to swing the racket toward impact. After the player in Figure 5.15 begins the forward transfer of linear momentum and steps toward the ball contact point, the hips begin to rotate. They in turn cause the trunk to rotate. The arms of both

a   b   c

Figure 5.15 Compare the hip and trunk movement in a two-handed backhand with that of the one-handed backhand seen in Figure 5.14. Observe the amount of hip rotation that occurs in (c) while the shoulders bring the arms and racket toward the impact point.

limbs rotate with the trunk, whereas no movement occurs at the elbows or wrists up to impact. That is, the trunk and arms rotate as one body part. After impact any number of contortions occur for the follow-through, depending on each player's idiosyncrasies. The most common follow-through is to wrap the arm and racket over the shoulder.

Dr. Jack's Tennis Tips

When swinging the racket for a two-handed backhand, do not try to drive the racket with your hands. This usually causes excessive wrist action and loss of shot control. Instead, think of driving the ball with your shoulders.

Our statement about a wrist flick in either stroke can now be discussed. Slight wrist movement does occur in a skilled one-handed backhand, but little is seen in the two-handed backhand. I must add, however, that all the players in my study were hitting down-the-line backhands. You may see more (but not a lot more) wrist motion in both strokes when going crosscourt. My suggestion is to keep the wrist (or wrists) firm in both strokes and forget about flicking the ball crosscourt.

Ease of Skill Acquisition

Which backhand is easier to learn? It seems that a player may be able to develop the skills to hit an effective two-handed backhand more readily. If you have to learn one of two strokes and you know that all characteristics of each stroke are similar except that one only uses two major body parts and the other uses five, which do you think would be easier to learn? And what if you learn to play with a two-handed backhand and wish to change later to a one-handed backhand? Almost any certified teaching professional can help you change strokes later, so develop your foundational skills first with whichever stroke you choose and then work on a change later if you so desire.

NET RESULTS

Both the one-handed and two-handed backhands have specific characteristics that are conducive to optimal performance. However, as you determine what would be the best for you and your game, consider some of the attributes listed in Table 5.1. With these concepts in mind, decide what areas give you the most problem when playing. You may even want to write down how the use of either a one- or two-handed backhand would help or hurt your own game. It is really an individual choice.

In my opinion, the two-handed backhand can be an incredibly powerful stroke. I feel also that it can be learned much easier than its counterpart. Many people have downplayed the two-hander because of its lack of reach; however, this criticism seems unjustified. The stroke not only provides you with a greater ability to hit topspin and high-bouncing balls, but it also allows you to use more trunk rotation in generating force to hit the ball. In addition, the two-handed stroke allows the shock of impact to be split up and absorbed by two arms instead of one. Many think the two-handed backhand is a fad or a psychological placebo that gives more confidence. I think it can serve as an asset to a player's game—the stroke is here to stay. If you don't believe it, look at Chang, Agassi, Seles, and Capriati—their two-handers are pretty good weapons.

Table 5.1   Comparison of One-Handed and Two-Handed Backhand

Characteristic	One-handed backhand	Two-handed backhand
Number of body parts used	Five—hips, trunk, arm, forearm, and hand	Two—hips, trunk and arms (as one unit)
Spin production	Underspin easy; topspin can cause problems	Topspin easy; underspin can cause problems
Disguise	Similar	Similar
Strength	More required because of one-arm involvement	Less required because of two-arm involvement
Grip change	Not absolutely necessary but is recommended	You can select a slight change or no change
Reach	Similar when you get adequately prepared and properly positioned	Similar when you get adequately prepared and properly positioned
Low returns (ankle high)	Easier to retrieve	You usually must use one hand
High-bouncing balls (head high or slightly above)	Easy but usually you must use underspin	Easy to hit flat or with topspin

C H A P T E R 6

Ball Spin:
Why, When, and How

There is only one way to produce ball spin in tennis. You must accelerate the racket head through impact to brush the backside of the ball in one of three ways:

1. Upward for topspin
2. Downward for underspin
3. Sideways for sidespin

The more vertical (or horizontal) you swing the racket (in either direction), the more ball spin you'll produce. The angle of the racket face at impact may have some influence on the amount of spin, but it will primarily determine the direction of ball flight off the racket.

The amount of spin a player imparts on the ball, combined with a high stroke velocity, often determines how effective the player will be. For example, Bjorn Borg has always been considered the master of topspin. If you had the chance to watch him play on television, you probably heard the announcers speak of his tremendous looping topspin shots and how difficult it was for the opponent to return any of those shots effectively. In contrast, Chris Evert could hit incredible sidespin on her forehand; Steffi Graf uses a great deal of underspin on her backhand; and Jimmy Connors has always played with very little spin. What is it, then, about spin that makes each player's style a winning one?

Spin can be used for various reasons. Some players like to use underspin (or backspin) because they feel they can better control shot placement. Sometimes, however, an underspin shot cannot be hit with great force (as in a passing shot) and still be controlled. Other players, who may attack the ball more aggressively, utilize topspin. They seem to hit balls that would normally fly beyond the baseline but don't because of the imparted topspin. Still other competitors use sidespin on some strokes, especially on the serve. Because so many variations of ball spin exist, you need to learn about spin and why it's so important in championship tennis.

The Effect of Spin on Ball Flight

As a tennis ball travels toward the opponent, its flight is affected by the surrounding air. Air turbulence creates tiny eddies around and behind the ball that cause it to slow down. When the ball is spinning, the air has an even more significant effect on ball flight. A ball with topspin rotates in the direction in which it travels and the spin carries with it a small boundary layer of air (Figure 6.1). On the side where the boundary layer is opposite to the oncoming air, a high-pressure area is built up (Figure 6.2). On the opposite side of the ball the two air flows are in the same direction and the velocity of the oncoming air is slightly increased, causing a low-pressure area. The ball tends to move toward the side where the least pressure exists. With topspin, pressure is greater on top

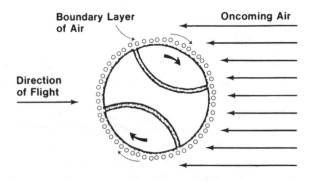

Figure 6.1   As the ball encounters the oncoming air, a small boundary layer of air travels around the ball as it spins.

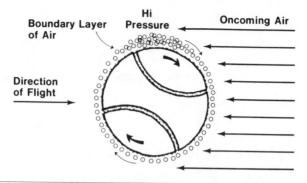

Figure 6.2   The boundary layer of air being carried around the ball in topspin direction interacts with the oncoming air to create a high-pressure zone above the ball.

of the ball and reduced under the ball, forcing it to drop more rapidly than normal. That's why a heavy topspin shot has such a looping trajectory. With underspin (Figure 6.3) the opposite occurs: Greater pressure is underneath the ball, keeping it in the air longer, causing the softly hit ball to "float" and the harder hit ball to "sail."

Just as ground strokes are most often hit with either underspin or topspin, the majority of serves are hit with varying types of sidespin. As seen in Figure 6.4, the rotation on a served ball ranges (for right-handed players) from a 3-o'clock sidespin on the ball to an almost 12-o'clock topspin. In flight, the ball with sidespin acts the same as a baseball pitcher's curve ball. It travels in a curved path opposite the side of the

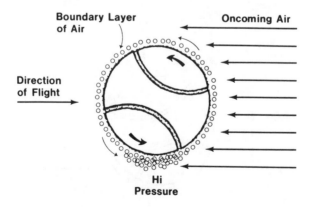

Figure 6.3   When the ball has underspin, the boundary layer travels around the ball in the direction of the underspin, creating a violent interaction beneath the ball. This interaction creates a high-pressure zone under the ball.

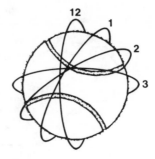

Figure 6.4 This figure depicts the types of ball spin that can usually be imparted. Note that a 12-o'clock spin is topspin, whereas a 3-o'clock spin is sidespin.

ball where the high-pressure zone is created (Figure 6.5). In fact, if a right-handed player imparts an extreme amount of sidespin (3-o'clock spin), the ball might deviate several feet to the left of the path it would have taken if no spin were hit.

In summary, consider a hypothetical situation (Figure 6.6) in which three ground strokes are hit with identical velocity and trajectory but with different types of spin. Let's assume a ball hit with no spin will land halfway between the service line and baseline. Relatively speaking, a ball with topspin will land near the service line, and a shot with underspin will bounce near the baseline. The flight of a ball hit with sidespin will be affected in a sideways trajectory and will curve either toward the middle of the court or toward the sideline.

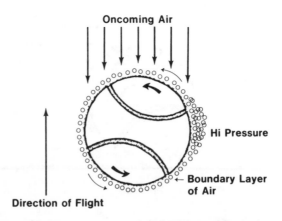

Figure 6.5 When a ball is hit with sidespin the high pressure zone is created where the turbulence occurs between the boundary layer of air and the oncoming air.

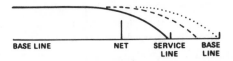

Figure 6.6 If three balls are hit from the same height at the same velocity with the same angle of departure from the racket, their flight patterns might differ as shown here. If a ball with no spin (- -) lands halfway between the service line and baseline, a ball with topspin (—) would bounce shorter into the opponent's court whereas a ball with underspin (. . .) would land farther into the opponent's court.

The Effect of Spin on Ball Bounce

Spin also affects how the ball bounces. Do you remember from high-school physics that if you look into a mirror at an oblique angle, you see something across the room that's situated at the same angle to the mirror as you? Similarly, if two people stand equidistant to and at the same angle from a mirror and both look toward the mirror's center, they will see each other. In theory, a tennis ball will bounce in the same manner if it has no spin. That is, the angle of the bounce from the court surface will be similar to the angle of approach to the tennis court. Due to frictional factors and the coefficient of restitution between the ball and tennis court, however, the angle of rebound is almost always greater than the approach angle.

Spin causes the ball to bounce much differently. For instance, the rotation on a ball with topspin pushes backward against the court, causing the ball to rebound at a lower angle than a ball with no spin (Figure 6.7).

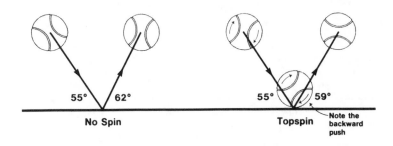

Figure 6.7 Compare the angle of rebound for a ball with topspin to the angle of a ball with no spin. There is a slight backward push by the spinning ball, which causes its rebound angle to be slightly less than the rebound of a ball with no spin.

That may be hard for you to believe, especially considering that all of Borg's opponents used to hit their returns of his topspin shots at about head height every time. It's true that Borg's shots often bounced higher than one would normally expect, which has in the past been attributed to the immense amount of topspin on the ball. To explain this phenomenon, I must mention two things. First, remember that topspin makes the ball bounce at a lower angle than a ball with no spin only when the angles of approach to the surface are identical. Second, a topspin drive causes the ball to loop over the net, and this looping effect forces the ball to strike the surface at a much steeper angle than would a ball without spin. Therefore, the explanation for Borg's high-bouncing topspin forehand lies in the ball's sharp approach angle to the court. If a spinless ball bounced on the court at the same angle of approach and with the same velocity as one with topspin, the spinless ball would bounce at a greater angle to the court surface.

The bounce of a ball hit with underspin is different from that of a ball hit with topspin. Whereas a topspin shot causes the ball to bounce at a lower angle than a ball with no spin, the rotation on the ball with underspin causes it to bounce at a greater angle under certain conditions. When the ball approaches the court at an angle of 45 degrees or greater, the underspin causes the ball to push forward during contact with the court, which forces the ball to slow down and rebound more vertically than normal. Figure 6.8 illustrates the different bounces caused by no spin and by underspin. Though the two balls approach the surface at the same angle, the one with underspin tends to grab the court and bounce at a steeper angle. A variety of circumstances can also cause a tennis ball to bounce differently. For instance, the slower the court surface (the grainer it is to "grab" the ball), the greater the effect of the spin on the bounce. On clay or Har-Tru (an artificial clay surface), the ball with

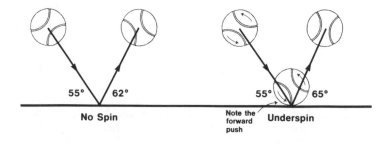

Figure 6.8   Notice the effect that underspin can have on the rebound of a tennis ball. There is a slight forward push by the spinning ball against the court, which causes its rebound angle to be slightly greater than that of a ball with no spin.

underspin will tend to stop and sit up (or bounce more vertically). On grass it will skid and rebound very low and fast.

The angle at which the underspin shot hits the court surface will also affect the rebound. High-speed film analyses demonstrates that a soft, lazy ground stroke hit with underspin will cause the shot to sit up, giving the opponent a chance for an easy return. A sliced drive that just clears the net will usually skid and take a low bounce, forcing the opponent to bend his or her knees to hit the return. This difference in rebound is caused by the angle of approach to the surface. In general, when the angle is greater than 45 degrees, the ball with underspin will bounce more vertically. When the ball hits the court at less than 45 degrees, it will usually skid and stay very low (Figure 6.9). Therefore, the intent of most underspin ground strokes is to drive the ball deep into the opponent's court with a low trajectory, forcing the opponent to hit up for net clearance. When John McEnroe, for example, decides to go to the net on a short shot that bounces below net level, he'll seldom use a topspin approach shot but will usually chip the ball with underspin. When you hit the underspin approach shot with a low trajectory, its approach angle to the court will be low, causing it to skid and remain low after the bounce. This forces the opponent to hit upward on the ball so it will clear the net, thus bettering your chances for a put-away volley. If, however, the chip shot goes too high over the net, the approach angle to the court will be too steep and the ball will take a high bounce, giving the opponent a chance at an easy winner. It's therefore imperative not to hit an underspin ground stroke too high over the net.

When the ball served with sidespin bounces, it can take several paths, depending on the type of ball spin. The ball hit with a 3-o'clock or 2-o'clock spin will tend to continue in its original curved path once it bounces. That is, the spin actually has little effect on the bounce in terms

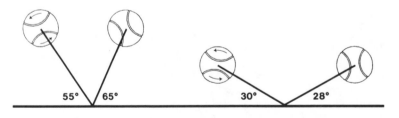

Figure 6.9 Observe how the rebound of a ball with underspin can be affected by its approach angle to the tennis court. Generally, if the ball with underspin approaches the court at an angle greater than 45 degrees, the result is a greater rebound angle. However, when the ball with underspin approaches the tennis court at an angle less than 45 degrees, the rebound is occasionally less than the approach angle.

of changing the ball's velocity or height of bounce. A ball with a 1-o'clock spin (somewhat of a combination of topspin and sidespin) will tend to bounce in a direction opposite to that of ball flight (depending on the court surface). The slower the court (e.g., clay), the more effect the spin will have, causing the ball to bounce in the direction opposite to ball flight. On a fast court surface (e.g., grass), however, the spin's effect will be lessened and the ball's bounce won't be as severe. If the bounce can cause the ball to deviate extremely from its flight path, this serve type can be very effective, especially as a second serve.

Application of Spin

Because ball spin can be used to vary the pace of a rally or keep the opponent from getting grooved to one type of ball bounce, spin must become an integral part of any player's repertoire. The problem now is how to apply spin.

Three techniques for the application of topspin have been popular in the past.

1. Swinging upward with a vertical racket face to brush the backside of the ball, keeping the wrist and elbow fairly firm (Figure 6.10)
2. Swinging the racket similarly but employing movement at the elbow and wrist, which accelerates the racket head more vertically (Figure 6.11)

Figure 6.10 Note that topspin can be hit by swinging in low-to-high fashion while employing little wrist or elbow movement.

Figure 6.11   This sequence shows a player hitting extremely heavy topspin.

3. Rotating the hand, forearm, and shoulder at contact, trying to roll the racket face over the ball (Figure 6.12)

a   b

Figure 6.12   This player attempts to roll the racket over the ball. Due to the time period of impact, rolling the racket face over the ball is virtually impossible.

Because many coaches have contradictory theories about topspin, I decided to investigate the two major elements of spin production: the linear motion of the racket in imparting spin, and the rotation of the racket prior to contact, at contact, and after contact. A high-speed camera shooting pictures at 500 frames per second was used to film 30 skilled players as they hit flat shots (with no spin), shots with topspin, and underspin shots.

It is extremely difficult to hit a ball completely without spin. The players all swung slightly upward (Figure 6.13) when attempting to hit a flat ball; the reasons for this are twofold.

1. The swing must be directed upward for the ball to clear the net; if a completely horizontal swing is used, the ball will never make it over.
2. To hit a spinless shot, the player must negate the forward spin of the approaching ball, which can be accomplished with an upward swing.

When comparing the two lines for no spin and topspin in Figure 6.13, you can see that the swings of these players became almost twice as steep

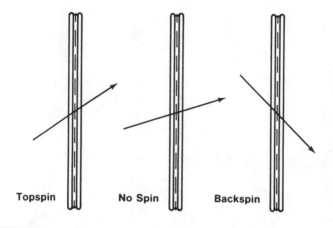

Figure 6.13   Notice how the linear motion of the racket head differs for hitting various ball spins. The angle of racket head motion when hitting topspin is almost twice as steep as that for hitting no spin. The angle of the racket head movement when hitting backspin (underspin) is in a steep downward direction.

when hitting topspin. This tells us that the linear motion of the racket head is important in spin production. In addition, two other points should be discussed. First, the more vertically the athlete accelerated the racket, the more spin was produced. Second, in contradiction to one of the previously mentioned theories on topspin production, none of the players rotated the racket head in their attempts to put additional spin on the ball. Following impact, however, racket head rotation was seen in many of the strokes. One reason for this rotation could be off-center ball contact on the racket face, which was seen in about 95 percent of the impacts. When a ball hits below or above the center of the racket, as shown in Figure 6.14, torque is created, forcing the racket head to rotate.

In Figure 6.13, you can also observe the steep downward action to produce underspin. The racket was always close to vertical (never being more than 5 to 7 degrees) and no racket rotation occurred until after the ball had been hit.

Another reason for racket head rotation is that as the arm and hand cross the body, they naturally rotate so the palm of the hand faces down. Place a racket in your hand, and the racket rolls over with the hand. This action is caused by the structure of the shoulder and does not occur until the arm crosses the body, obviously well after a tennis ball is hit.

Regardless of the reason for its occurrence, no racket head rotation contributed to ball spin; by the time any rotation did occur, the ball was

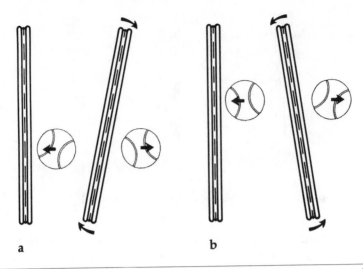

Figure 6.14 You can see how a torque is created from off-center impacts below the central axis of the racket (a) and above the central axis of the racket (b).

clearly off the racket and on its way back over the net. Therefore, the rotation of the racket face couldn't possibly have affected the amount of spin on the ball. The racket face at impact was usually very close to being vertical. This tells us that the angle of the racket face plays only a minor role in imparting topspin, a conclusion that may cause some skepticism, because we've all seen professional players apply topspin by seeming to roll the racket over the ball. But the facts remain; it just doesn't happen.

Hitting Topspin

If rolling the racket face is not the way to produce topspin, how is it done? Let's assume that you are standing at the baseline in your ready position, holding the grip of your racket with your normal hand and keeping your opposite hand at the throat. As soon as you see the ball come off the opponent's racket and travel toward your forehand side, employ the unit turn and help take the racket back with your opposite hand (Figure 6.15). Just prior to initiating the forward swing, step toward the ball (or use an open stance if you prefer) and then swing upward to establish contact just in front of your body. End your follow-through high above your head. At first, you should keep your wrists and elbows firm when hitting topspin. Once you develop the precise timing, you can try to gain additional spin by employing various wrist and elbow movements to accelerate the racket head more vertically.

a   b

Figure 6.15   Notice the low-to-high racket action used to hit a topspin forehand.

Dr. Jack's Tennis Tips

- When hitting topspin, think of aggressively brushing the back of the ball upward, trying to make it revolve around a fixed axis. Once you learn how to spin the ball, immediately work on hitting your topspin shots deep into the opponent's court.
- If you have trouble hitting topspin, try "crowding" the ball (or getting a little closer to it) just a bit. This decreases the length of the lever (your reach) and will allow you to rotate your trunk faster.
- Do what Laver says he did when the pressure was on. He would actually swing harder with a more vertically upward swing to hit more topspin, trying to keep the ball in the court.

Hitting Underspin

To hit a ball with underspin, you must strike the backside of the ball in a downward fashion (Figure 6.16). Past coaching has produced several methods of hitting underspin that are similar to those suggested for topspin, the most ludicrous being to turn the racket under the ball at impact. Our study of the 30 highly skilled players clearly indicated that underspin can be imparted only by brushing the backside of the ball in a downward manner with the racket face slightly open, as you see in Figure 6.16.

Now, it's true that whenever a pro hits an underspin backhand, the racket seems to turn under the ball at contact and continue to turn after the ball leaves the racket. Remember that the time of ball contact is so short that it's impossible to rotate the racket head fast enough to aid in spin production. One reason the racket may turn is that it's natural in the follow-through position for the hand and forearm to turn so the palm

a   b

c

Figure 6.16   Here you can see how to hit a two-handed backhand drive with underspin.

faces downward (the same thing happened during the follow-through when players hit a lot of topspin). Another reason for the turning effect may be the force produced by the ball on the racket face.

In almost all of the 30 cases studied the ball contacted the racket in the hitting zone slightly above the center, causing the racket to rotate as shown in Figure 6.14b. To hit an underspin shot, you must take the racket back higher than you would for a routine ground stroke. With the racket head turned slightly open, you must swing downward to hit the ball. Don't chop at the ball, but drive slightly downward until after ball contact. At this point, a pro will usually move the racket up around shoulder height. This is a rhythmic motion that isn't really necessary for everyone. The downward swing, however, is essential to hit underspin. The open racket face simply combines with the downward swing to send the ball over the net. Just be careful not to open the racket face too much, causing the underspin shot to have a high trajectory and allowing the ball to sit up for the opponent. Kept low and deep, underspin becomes a useful weapon.

Dr. Jack's Tennis Tips

When hitting an underspin drive, try to knife the ball with a long follow-through toward the net. This will insure a high racket head velocity through impact.

Which Is Easier to Hit: Topspin or Underspin?

In which case (topspin or underspin) do you think more rotation can be put on the ball? This question may sound a little ridiculous, but the answer actually plays a big role in controlling a tennis shot. Here's a clue to the answer: What type of spin do most players resort to when the pressure in a match gets tight? Although not everyone does it, many competitors (especially the nervous ones) use underspin in these situations and they don't even know why. To help you understand the reason, think how a ball rotates following its bounce from the court; 99.9 percent of the time it has topspin (Figure 6.17). However, imagine that you have just hit that ball (which came toward you with topspin) and it's spinning the same way as it heads toward your opponent. Now the topspin, as you viewed it before you hit the ball, is underspin. Therefore, when you hit a topspin return, you must stop the spin already on the ball from the bounce and change it so the ball rotates in the opposite direction. When you place underspin on the ball you merely add to

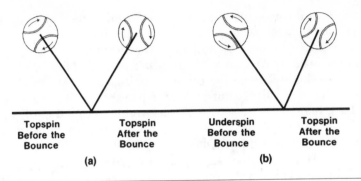

| Topspin Before the Bounce | Topspin After the Bounce | Underspin Before the Bounce | Topspin After the Bounce |
| (a) | | (b) | |

Figure 6.17 Notice in these two conditions how a ball, with initial topspin (a) or underspin (b), has topspin following the rebound.

what's already there. That's why it's an easier shot to hit when the pressure's on!

NET RESULTS

A mastery of spin production is a necessity if you want to play championship tennis. To prevent your opponent from getting grooved to your strokes, you must be able to vary ball spins. In doing so, you can keep the opponent off balance and also prevent him or her from easily setting up to tee off on your shots. Remember, however, that your opponent will also try to do the same thing. Therefore, the mastery of spin not only includes the ability to hit various spins but also to read the trajectory of the opponent's shot and prepare according to how it will bounce toward you.

C H A P T E R 7

Making a Good Volley Even Better

All skilled tennis players know how to volley, probably because very little racket movement is required, making the volley a fairly simple shot to hit. However, many volleys lack the velocity, depth, and penetration necessary for championship tennis. Some tennis players may not realize the difference between a punch volley and a drive volley, how crucial the timing is on the split step prior to volleying, or what the trajectory of the ball off the racket should be. This chapter will address these topics and more.

Causes of Poor Volleys

We should first discuss two major causes of poor volleys: overemphasis on developing ground strokes while learning to play, and fear of being at the net.

Many world-class players, such as Andre Agassi, Michael Chang, and Steffi Graf, are renowned for their effective ground strokes but not for their volleys. Although all of these athletes have excellent volleys, you seldom see them at the net because their strengths have always been in their ground strokes. Because they don't practice volleying as much as someone like Navratilova or McEnroe, their timing skills at the net aren't as good as they could be. Realizing this, some tennis players tend to lose confidence in their volleys during important points. Once when Andrea Jaeger beat Chris Evert in the finals of a major tournament, she was asked what her basic strategy was. Her reply was, "I wanted to be patient and wait for her to make a mistake. I really didn't want to go to the net or do something else that was stupid." Jaeger showed a great deal of respect for Evert's ground strokes, and she knew her own ground strokes were her strongest attributes. However, a person with an aggressive approach shot and volley may have been able to end the points a bit easier; thus we see the need to develop all aspects of your game.

Another cause of problematic volleys is fear, which you can understand if you imagine yourself in a baseline rally. As you and your opponent hit the ball from baseline to baseline, the ball travels at least 78 feet. You have time to read the opponent's shot, decide what you intend to do with the ball, move into position, and hit the proper stroke following the bounce. Suddenly you realize the opponent has hit a short ball inside the service line, so you hit an approach shot, hoping to gain a more strategic position at the net. As the opponent hits the return of your approach shot, the ball travels only about 50 feet toward you, and you need to hit a volley. It's not easy to follow the ball's trajectory and your timing must change drastically from a routine ground stroke at the baseline to the quick reaction and movement of volleying at the net. With all these sudden changes in timing and preparation, we can see why some people fear the net position and how difficult it is for them to volley well during a point.

Footwork Is Crucial on the Volley

As with other strokes in tennis, a good volley begins with proper footwork. Volley footwork is different than footwork on the other strokes because the body often doesn't turn as much and because the volley is a much shorter stroke that requires less ground reaction force than ground strokes. However, positioning is still crucial. If you're not in position to hit an offensive volley, you'll have to settle for a more defensive shot to keep the ball in play. This gives your opponent one more chance to hit a winner. So let's talk about proper footwork for the volley.

Getting to the Net: The Split Step

There are two ways to get to the net: serve and volley, or hit an approach shot and advance toward the net. Whichever method you employ, you must use the same footwork as you near the volleying position. This is the split step, a step that resembles a movement in hopscotch. We've all seen the pros perform it. For example, when John McEnroe hits a serve in doubles (Figure 7.1) he follows it in, and as the opponent begins his forward swing, McEnroe spreads his legs slightly (but keeps them parallel with his shoulders) to land in somewhat of a ready position awaiting the opponent's return. This ready position or split step may be the single most overlooked part of volleying.

a   b

c   d

Figure 7.1   John McEnroe has an excellent serve-and-volley maneuver. Notice the split step occurring just prior to the volley in (d).

What is the purpose of the split step? Is it to become stable in a ready position so you can move with equal quickness in all directions? That's partially the answer, but there's much more to hitting a great volley. It's true that as a skilled tennis player split steps we see the feet go apart, but this position is not static once the player lands. The feet do not simply go apart, land, and stay in that location until the swing is initiated. In fact, the body's center of gravity keeps moving forward even though the feet plant for an instant. When the feet separate to split step, they should generate an elastic quality and bounce out of the split step and into the volley. If no bounce occurs, the ankles and knees will become major shock absorbers and flex significantly. This will force the player to sink deeper into a crouch position and will hinder quick reactions.

Timing the Split Step

Timing is crucial with this move. Players who go into the split step too soon will bounce out of it too quickly, readying themselves for the volley too early for an effective momentum transfer. Players who initiate the split step too late look as though they are running through the volley, causing poor body balance and extremely poor shot control. As a general rule, you should split step as your opponent begins the forward swing. Although not a scientifically valid way of determining when to split step, this is a good practice because it usually will allow you to split step and hit a well-timed volley. In fact (just to give you a little scientific tidbit), my colleagues and I used high-speed film to evaluate the mechanics of the split step. We found that the great volleyers actually split step during the instant just after the opponent's impact. This means that through trial and error, they learned exactly when the split step must occur to get them to the net as quickly as possible and still allow their brains to have enough time to process the impact and give the signal to move toward the volley position. However, I don't advise you try split stepping just after the opponent makes contact with the ball. The relationship between your eyes focusing on what's going on and your brain consciously trying to determine exactly when to land simply would create too many timing and movement problems. So, try landing on the split step just as the opponent makes contact with the ball. As your skill develops, you will probably begin landing a split second later and you won't even realize it!

Dr. Jack's Tennis Tips

If you have an excellent serve or a perfect approach shot and you see your opponent beginning to lunge at the ball, don't split step! The return will likely be weak, enabling you to rush in closer to the net.

Mechanics of the Split Step

The function of the split step is to widen the stance, creating a stable, yet not fixed, base of support upon landing. The wider and more stable the base (within reason), the faster you become unstable toward the direction of the unit turn movement. This allows very fast movements in any direction. The main point, then, is to properly time the split step action and create a slight imbalance forward in the direction of the volley.

Volleying From the Split Step

As you prepare to bounce out of the split step to hit the volley, always try to step forward into the shot, as shown in Figure 7.2. When you go

Figure 7.2   The player shows how to move forward when hitting a strong volley.

to the net, think of your parallel foot positioning in the split step as being the base of a triangle (Figure 7.3). As the ball approaches, step to the top of the triangle just before making contact with the ball. This will ensure a sound transfer of momentum into the stroke. One you hit the ball, maintain the base of the triangle position again. Obviously, at times this footwork will be impossible, such as when you get jammed by an opponent's stroke or when you must stretch to volley the return. However, if you understand and use this forward weight transfer, your volley should improve immensely.

Upper Body Mechanics in Volleying

Once you achieve the correct lower body movements, the upper body comes into play. If your footwork is precisely performed, the hips and

a

b

c

Figure 7.3   From the ready position (a) the player steps toward the top of the triangle (b) to volley the ball (c).

trunk will be turned slightly to accommodate a good volleying action. At this point, some tennis players make a serious mistake when volleying. They try to overpower the volley by using a full swing that severely hampers control.

Because hitting the volley with precision is obviously important, we next discuss the advantages and disadvantages of two distinctly different volley types: the punch volley and the drive volley. The punch volley, shown in Figure 7.4, refers to a short, compact volley that utilizes very little backswing or follow-through. The drive volley, seen in Figure 7.5, gets its name from an emphasized backswing and follow-through employed as the player drives the ball into the opponent's court. Timing is crucial when you volley and this is particularly true with the drive volley. The punch volley must also be a well-timed stroke, but because of the

a   b   c

Figure 7.4   This athlete shows the proper execution for a punch volley. Notice the slight backswing and short stroking maneuver used when contacting the ball.

a   b

Figure 7.5   This competitor demonstrates a drive volley. Compare the difference in the backswing and follow-through with those of the punch volley, seen in Figure 7.4.

longer upper limb movements required by the drive volley, timing is even more critical for the drive. To prove this fact and show how different skill levels are affected by these techniques, my colleagues and I conducted a study on the drive volley techniques of advanced, intermediate, and beginning players. All players were asked to stand in a specific spot on the court near the net and hit a drive volley directly back toward a target close to the baseline. They were filmed at 200 frames per second as they tried to hit drive volleys toward the target.

As we expected, the skilled players executed excellent drive volleys, hitting each ball near the racket face center. The intermediate players hit only mediocre drive volleys, and most impacts were off-center, causing a great deal of racket rotation. The beginners, needless to say, had their difficulties; very few of their drive volleys even made it over the net and all impacts were severely off center. Only one person hit the target, and interestingly enough it wasn't one of the advanced players. It was one of the beginners who, after becoming frustrated with drive volleys, used a punch volley. His first and only punch volley hit the target. Further investigation revealed that all the players had more control using a punch volley. Therefore, this study seems important in two respects: (1) only skilled players have the timing required to hit an effective drive volley, and even their control is suspect when using it, and (2) the punch volley may provide a player with a good deal more control than the drive volley.

Arm Movement in Effective Volleying

Regardless of whether a drive or punch volley is used, the arm motions of some tennis players can still cause some serious accuracy problems. As players bounce into and out of the split step, they often hold their elbows close to their bodies. This can slow down a player's racket work tremendously. In fact, I'm sure you've heard how some players are said to have quick hands at the net because they react to high-velocity shots so well. The hands may have something to do with it, but the real key lies in the upper limb positioning. When the elbows are held in tight to the body, the upper limb must rotate outward. The racket actually goes into a slight backswing position that, for many players, can cause late ball contact and poor control. If the elbows are held slightly away from the body, the upper limb can be used a bit more effectively, and less rotation at the shoulder will occur. This means the racket will not go into a backswing position but will stay in front of the body. This allows for more effective impact and enables the player to have quicker hands than if the elbows are held in.

Quick hands are necessary when you react to a ball that hits the net tape. When this occurs the ball usually stays on the opponent's side of the court and you win the point. At times, however, the ball will hit the net tape and continue toward you in one of two ways: (1) It will tip the net tape and skip slightly upward, losing little velocity, or (2) it will hit the tape solidly and barely fall over into your court. When you hear the ball hit the tape, you must react quickly: Either (1) lift the racket head slightly so if the ball skips up off the net you will have a chance to contact it, or (2) immediately sprint forward so you can hit the ball before it bounces twice. Although these two phenomena don't happen often in a tennis match, I've seen a lot of points won by a player merely reacting to one of these situations. Remember, your opponent isn't intentionally trying to hit the net tape, so whenever the ball hits the net and comes into your court, your opponent is usually caught off guard and must react with you.

What Grip to Use When Volleying

We've studied the importance of proper footwork and body mechanics in hitting volleys, so the next step is to analyze how the racket should be held. This may seem trivial to some players, but how the racket is oriented in the hand will have a huge effect on how well the ball is hit and where it will go once hit. Two trains of thought exist when prescribing the grips to use when volleying: (1) Change grips from an eastern forehand grip for a forehand volley to an eastern backhand grip for a backhand volley, and (2) use a continental grip for volleys on both sides. The primary goal of each technique is to provide the player with a comfortable grip that provides a nearly flat racket face at impact. There are biomechanical advantages and disadvantages related to either gripping technique, and for quite some time authorities have debated which grip provides the greatest advantages for volleying.

Tennis authorities over the years have been split not only between which gripping method is best for the beginning player but also between when technique seems most appropriate as skill rises. Three major schools of thought on teaching exist.

1. If the player learns the continental grip in the early stages of playing and uses it throughout his or her career, the player has a better chance for advanced stroke development.
2. The eastern grip change is best taught to the beginners, who should use this technique for the duration of their careers.
3. The eastern grip method is best used to teach the novice player, but the player should change to the continental grip as skill develops.

This diversity of opinion has made the decision of which method to use a difficult one for any player. Therefore, we need to examine specifically what the experts say about the use of each grip. Then we can apply sports science concepts to the controversy to help you make certain decisions about what is best for you.

Those who support the continental grip (Figure 7.6) point to several advantages of this technique, the most popular claim being the time factor involved when compared with the eastern grip change. Because the time needed for stroke preparation is reduced when the player is at the net, proponents feel that the continental grip requires less time to execute an effective volley. This group also cites that the player using a continental grip need only be concerned about the gripping method, which seems desirable in pressure situations. Another claim favoring use of the continental grip is that it provides for a greater degree of adaptability

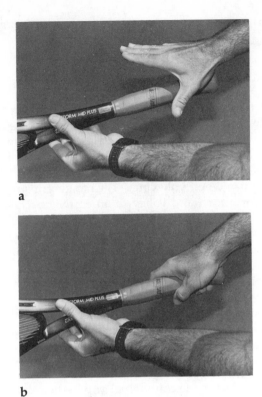

a

b

Figure 7.6   Notice how the V of the hand is located over the inside beveled (angled) edge of the racket handle when the player uses a continental grip.

on the part of the player. This technique naturally permits an open racket face, which assists in handling low balls, and some feel that the open racket face is most adaptable for the various reaction-type situations that occur in net play. Still others claim that the player's comfort and confidence are improved by using the continental grip (because no grip change is required), thus improving play at the net.

The second school of thought regarding the volley grip includes those coaches who support the notion that the eastern grip-change method is best for the advanced player. Most of these authorities feel there is plenty of time, even in the quickest of net volley exchanges, to make the grip change from forehand (Figure 7.7a and b) to backhand (Figure 7.7c and d). They note that if the grip change is the first move on the player's part, time does not become a factor. These individuals have cited many mechanical advantages corresponding to the eastern grips that make them seem to be the superior choice. These proponents feel that this grip offers increased control on high volleys, better directional control down the line, and greater strength (due to how the hand is oriented on the handle) for the volley.

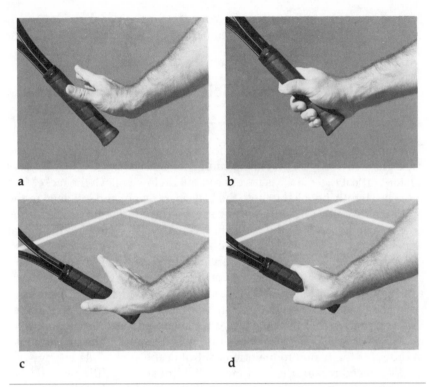

a   b

c   d

Figure 7.7   Note the placement of the V of the hand to form the eastern forehand (a and b) and eastern backhand (c and d).

Still other tennis experts suggest teaching beginners and advanced beginners the eastern grip-change method but having the students switch to the continental grip as their skills improve. These experts agree that the beginning player must first learn to develop a vertical racket face at impact, but as advancements are made in skill the student should modify the hand position on the racket to the continental grip. By doing so, the advanced player can take advantage of the slightly open-faced racket and time-saving characteristics. Some veteran tennis instructors feel that the beginner's level of play allows time for a pivot and grip change, but as play becomes quicker with increased skill level, the player needs to use the no-change advantage of the continental grip. Some authorities even point out that the player may have plenty of time for a grip change at the elite level of competition but that problems often arise due to the difficulty in locating the proper hand position for the eastern grip change. Another problem that arises is that the student becomes so comfortable with the grip he or she first uses that the habit is difficult to change later.

Much of the previous information has been derived through the personal experiences and observations of individuals who play or teach professionally. Their ideas are sound, but we might be able to go a step further by applying sport science concepts to the problems involved. Therefore, let's analyze what goes into the grip of a mechanically efficient volley.

What Sport Science Tells Us About the Volley Grip

The most important requirement for a volley grip is that it orient the racket face correctly so that an optimum shot can be hit. On high volleys a near-vertical racket face is necessary, but on low volleys the racket face must be slightly beveled to help the ball clear the net and fall deep in the opponent's court. One difference between the continental grip and the eastern grip lies in how the racket face is naturally oriented to the ball at impact. The eastern grip allows the wrist to be in a mechanically sound confirmation and easily presents a vertical racket face to the ball at impact. This allows for a direct force transfer from racket to ball and ensures a firm, high-velocity shot if desired. Contrary to this, the continental grip normally causes some wrist deviation if used properly and also causes the racket face to be slightly beveled backward so it is open to the ball at impact. This assists the player in putting underspin on the ball, because in order for the player to maintain control of the shot while hitting with an open-faced racket, the stroking motion must be slightly high to low. Interestingly enough, it can be argued that both grip techniques enhance volley control, the eastern grip because it provides optimal ball–racket impact and the continental grip because it allows for underspin to be used readily and helps with shot depth due to the open face.

One of the most often mentioned disadvantages of the continental grip is the difficulty it causes a player in volleying down the line on the forehand side while at a position near the service line. This inside-out shot has been a topic of concern. If you use an eastern forehand grip (Figure 7.8) it is fairly easy to go down the line without any significant wrist or elbow contortions. If you use a continental grip, you must maneuver the wrist and elbow into the proper positions or else utilize the unit turn and orient the body so the upper limb won't have to go through these motions.

Another mechanical advantage favoring the eastern grip change involves the backhand volley, in which an eastern backhand grip allows the wrist to be in an efficient position. In contrast, a backhand volley with a continental grip places a great deal of muscular stress on the forearm. From a sports medicine point of view, this evidence alone favors use of the eastern grip change, and, in fact, very few tennis players actually use a true continental grip for both the forehand and backhand volley.

Figure 7.8 The inside-out volley can be hit a little easier with an eastern forehand grip (a) than with a continental grip (b).

Although most pros using the continental grip feel they do not change grips between these two volleys, evidence suggests that some form of grip change almost always occurs. As a player prepares for a backhand volley, the thumb and forefinger remain in place on the racket handle but there is a slight shift of the heel and hand toward the inside (Figure 7.9). If you have problems understanding why this slight hand shift occurs, try hitting both forehand and backhand volleys with a true continental grip. If sufficient strength isn't present in the wrist extensors (on the back of the forearm), you will most likely experience a great deal of stress in the forearm during the backhand volley. If you use a hand shift, the angle of pull of these muscles is reduced so the stress isn't as great.

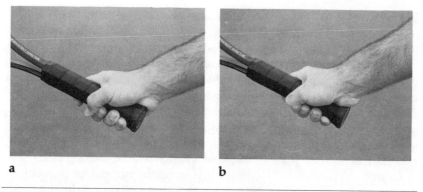

Figure 7.9 Observe how the heel of the hand shifts toward the inside when hitting a backhand volley with a continental grip.

If you question the time limitation of the slight hand shift in the continental grip, be aware that ample time does exist. The required movement is so small relative to the eastern grip changes that the continental grip hand shift can be made without the use of the opposite hand, whereas an eastern grip change almost always requires use of the opposite hand.

Based on the information available, I recommend that you use a continental grip on your forehand volley and employ the slight hand shift to hit a backhand volley. In almost all tennis situations, ample time exists for the hand shift to occur. In addition, it seems that the advantages of having a slightly open racket face outweigh the advantages of using a vertical racket face. As for control, both grips may be good but I feel the high-to-low racket action with the slightly open racket face necessitated by the continental grip allows for better placement and depth of volleys.

More on Volley Control

The discussion of control in volleying leads to four final points that will be listed here and then examined in depth later.

1. Be sure the racket face stays firm through impact, and avoid dishing it in an attempt to increase ball underspin.
2. When hitting low volleys try to get low (by bending your knees, not by bending at the waist) so your eyes are closer to the height of impact.
3. Never hit down on a high volley unless you are attempting to hit a short volley.
4. Avoid hitting low volleys whenever you can.

Avoid Dishing the Volley

Many players try dishing the ball when volleying, sometimes even without the player's awareness. In an attempt to place additional underspin on the ball, a player may use not only a slight high-to-low motion but also a dishing action that seems to roll the racket under and around the ball. From the chapter on spin production you should remember that the time limitations of impact won't allow you to dish the ball. A high-speed film analysis of highly skilled players shows that when they dish the racket, the dishing doesn't occur until after the ball has been hit. A more in-depth examination reveals that players who dish the ball employ no racket head rotation prior to ball contact and that the dishing effect seen is usually a reaction to the impact; it is not a purposeful movement. Therefore, hit your volleys with a firm racket. It's all right to let the racket dish once the ball has been hit, but use no racket rotation before contact, even on balls below the net tape.

Dr. Jack's Tennis Tips

To avoid dishing the racket before a volley impact, you can squeeze the grip just before striking the ball. Just be sure you're strong enough to do it volley after volley.

Low Volleys

Low volleys seem to cause a lot of headaches. Regardless of whether you hit the low volley long, into the net, or simply not well enough to suit you, one simple mechanical principle might help: It's fairly well accepted that you will be a more accurate player when your eyes are located near the point of contact. Obviously, some volleys are so low that it's impossible to get your head down that far. A good cue is to bend your knees to situate your seat as low as possible and get your eyes near the level of the volley. Tim Mayotte accomplishes this quite well, as you can see in Figure 7.10. Hitting low volleys like this will increase your accuracy and allow you to be a more offensive player at the net.

Figure 7.10   As Tim Mayotte demonstrates, it is important to get your body down on low volleys so your eyes are as near the level of impact as possible.

Don't Hit Down on a High Volley

Some players feel that an offensive volley should be hit hard and short into the opponent's court. Although these shots are sometimes effective, the volleys are usually so short in the opponent's court that any advantage gained by going to the net is lost because the opponent has too much time to read the volley, judge its bounce, move in, and hit the passing shot. The problem may stem from the fact that a player stands higher than the net and can see more of the opponent's court, which gives the player an unrealistic sense of depth into the opponent's court. Therefore, some players feel they must hit downward on each volley. This usually finds the volley in the net or so short in the court that it has little effect. These players don't realize that gravity can be of great assistance in tennis, and thus they don't let it work for them. I think all of us will agree that the deeper a volley is in the court the more effective it becomes (unless you want to hit short angles, of course). This means that you cannot hit the ball downward; you must direct it at least straight out from the racket face or even slightly upward. To get the feeling of how deep volleys should be hit, try volleying the ball long (out of the court) and then slowly try to bring the subsequent volley back into the court. Don't be concerned with velocity until you obtain good control. Once you develop a deep, controlled volley, you'll be amazed at how much more effective your net play will be.

Dr. Jack's Tennis Tips

When volleying for depth, again think of hitting three balls in a row straight out from the racket with a single stroke. The actual ball you're hitting is the first one; then pretend you're hitting two more deep into the court. This will ensure the proper follow-through essential for good depth volleys.

Always Try to Volley the Ball

Another facet of volleying that separates good volleyers from great volleyers is the point where the ball is contacted relative to the player's body. Many players, even though they may have excellent volleys, never perform to their potential at the net because they're lazy. These athletes will go to the net and hit a ball wherever it happens to be relative to their own bodies. In other words, they don't close in toward the net and attack the volley. Great players will always close in on opponents' shots, attempting to volley the shots before they drop below net height. By doing this players become more effective from two standpoints: They are closer to the net, thus minimizing the possibility of volleying the ball into the net, and they hit the ball at a higher point than they would if they waited for it to reach them in a position farther from the net. Both situations allow the volleyer to be a more offensive player. Therefore, be watchful for an opponent's lob, and whenever possible don't let an opponent's shot dip below the net and force you into a more defensive position.

Dr. Jack's Tennis Tips

When practicing your volley, work on two major goals: hitting the deep, penetrating volley and hitting the short, angled volley. They are all you'll ever need.

The Drop Volley

One of the most overused shots in tennis is the drop volley. It's a great shot to have in your repertoire, but many players use it too often. The purpose behind a good drop volley is to catch the opponent off guard when he or she is expecting a hard drive or to hit a winner when the opponent is pulled out of position. However, it is also a crowd pleaser. When hit properly, it comes across as a beautifully contrived work of art, receives many "oohs" and "ahs" from the crowd, and generally reinforces a tennis player's actions when at the net. The problem is that whenever a player hears the crowd's reaction to a beautiful drop volley, the player seems to do it again and again. After a while the opponent is actually waiting for the player to hit another drop volley so he or she can pounce on it.

Because most players tend to utilize the drop volley too much, I have developed a philosophy that I use often. To those players I say, "Don't hit a drop volley unless your opponent has fallen down and has one foot caught under the back fence." This usually makes a point that the drop shot should not be overused. However, when executed at the proper time, the drop volley can be a devastating weapon.

To hit an effective drop volley, you merely need to decelerate the racket head at impact. Remember that on a punch volley or a drive volley you are trying to sharply strike the ball and accelerate the racket head through impact. During the drop volley you must slow down the racket head as contact with the ball occurs. Players have different ways of doing this. Some soften the grip, whereas others drop the racket quickly as the ball contacts the racket head. I'm not sure I agree with either of these techniques. Your goal must be to slow down the racket head as you approach impact, but softening the grip or dropping the racket head at the last second may not really do that. One cue that may help you is to try to just touch the ball. As a goal, practice hitting your drop volley and making the ball bounce 5 times before it gets to the opponent's service line. In addition, don't hit the ball with a trajectory too high over the net. Remember that the higher the ball goes over the net, the more time the opponent has to react and run down your drop volley. You must strive for low net clearance and several bounces prior to reaching the opponent's service line.

In summary, remember that the drop volley should only be hit in specific situations. If the opponent is not out of position or caught off guard, any psychological momentum you gain from trying to hit the drop volley will be lost. Instead, the opponent will gain a great deal of psychological momentum in retrieving a shot that you thought was going to be a clear winner. Therefore, be smart, and learn to hit the drop volley in the proper manner and at the right time.

Dr. Jack's Tennis Tips

All too often a player relaxes mentally when hitting a drop volley. This is natural, because the ball is hit so softly. The result, however, is usually a poor shot or a mistake. That's why I say to maintain the same peak mental intensity to hit a delicate drop volley that you use to hit an overhead smash.

The Half Volley

Sometimes you can't avoid hitting a low shot when you are at the net. Although you should try to volley the ball whenever you can, you will encounter situations in which the ball will bounce first and you will have to hit what is known as a half volley. This short pickup stroke can be extremely effective, but the timing and mechanics are often very difficult. To hit a half volley you must use a very short backswing and contact the ball as it rises from the court (Figure 7.11). Guide the ball to the desired position in the opponent's court, usually short or deep and down the line.

Don't panic if you must hit a half volley. Think of it as a control shot. Used effectively, it can keep the opponent off balance and be an excellent weapon in your stroke repertoire.

Dr. Jack's Tennis Tips

When hitting a half volley, use a short backswing, a quick pickup stroke, and a lengthy follow-through.

a   b   c

Figure 7.11   The athlete demonstrates how a proper half volley should be performed. Notice how he meets the ball just as it rebounds from the court to guide it over the net.

NET RESULTS

It's important that you analyze everything relative to your own net play. Does the grip you use, combined with your volley mechanisms and footwork, allow you to hit deep, short, and angled shots with control? Also consider how balanced you are when approaching the net and during the split step. Be sure to transfer your body momentum forward in the correct manner and time it appropriately with your volley. Don't try to overpower the volley; use the velocity of the opponent's shot to your advantage and avoid extraneous racket head movement before ball contact. For high volleys, hit the ball straight out from the racket face unless you want to hit a short volley. For low volleys, get your seat and eyes low, near the level of impact. If you employ these characteristics in your net game, your volley should become a very penetrating weapon.

C H A P T E R   8

The Serve and Overhead: Your Ultimate Weapons

Serving a tennis ball and hitting an overhead smash are similar to pitching a baseball. When good leg action is synchronized with the proper upper body mechanics, these strokes can be devastating weapons. Many athletes, however, have trouble with these strokes because they either don't use their entire bodies to their advantage or they have poor timing between the various body segments. This creates even more problems for the player wishing to play championship tennis, because the serve and overhead are possibly the most important strokes in the game.

The serve starts every point in a game and can be very effective in helping you win a point, or it can be a back breaker in a match if it is not hit well. In other words, it can cause you to win or lose. The same can be said for the overhead smash. If you are in a position to hit an overhead, you have an edge over the opponent and should be able to attack with the smash. But if your overhead technique is poor and you can't hit the ball effectively, the opponent ends up with the psychological momentum and can take the offensive. Therefore, we will discuss the mechanical aspects of a skilled serve and overhead in terms of the force that must be generated and how that force is transferred through the body to the racket and ball.

Developing Force for the Serve and Overhead

Contrary to what many believe, the force provided by the body to hit a properly executed serve or overhead isn't developed at the trunk and upper limb. The majority of force is generated from the ground in the form of a ground reaction force. Remember Newton's third law: For every action, there is an equal and opposite reaction. When you serve or hit an overhead, your feet push against the ground and the ground pushes back with the same amount of force. Notice in Figure 8.1 how Ivan Lendl flexes and extends his knees to create a solid ground reaction force. Few tennis players use this principle to its fullest advantage. Obviously the one thing that will increase the ground reaction force is correct use of knee flexion and extension. Two problems often prevent players from correctly using the knees: too little or too much knee flexion, and improper timing of the knee movement relative to the rest of the stroke.

The proper amount of knee flexion actually depends on your strength and coordination. Consider this example: If you were trying to jump as high as possible vertically, would you bend your knees just a little or would you go into a deep crouch? I doubt you would do either. There is an optimum amount of knee flexion unique to each individual. Without enough knee bend you will generate poor ground reaction force, whereas too much knee flexion will result in excessive body motion and an inefficient transfer of force from the ground.

The second problem encountered by many tennis players is poor timing of the knee action relative to the entire serving or overhead motion. Remember that the segments of the body act as a system of chain links whereby the force generated by one link, or body part, is transferred in succession to the next link. When the transfer of that force is not efficient, the outcome of the stroke will be less than desirable. Because the knee bend is among the first of all body movements involved in the serve and overhead smash, it functions as the foundation for other segmental actions.

One instructional cue I use with the players I coach is telling them to flex their knees as the ball is tossed on the serve (Figure 8.2). As the athlete prepares to swing forward, I tell him or her to thrust and throw. The thrusting action causes the player to flex and then extend the legs forcefully toward the impact point, whereas the throwing action initiates the proper body rotation. You can use the same concept when hitting an overhead. Thus the force in serving and smashing is generated through a ground reaction force caused by knee flexion and extension. Once the knees extend, the sequencing of body parts begins with the first segment—the hips.

Figure 8.1   Ivan Lendl demonstrates how the knees should flex and extend when you hit an effective serve.

Dr. Jack's Tennis Tips

Here's a cue I have used successfully with some players wishing to use their legs on their serve. I tell them to think of sitting down as they toss the ball. Don't worry—there isn't enough time for you to go too low. Then, as you are ready to swing, explode up to the ball.

a

b   c

Figure 8.2 Notice how the knees are flexed as the ball toss is completed in (a). You can see in (b) and (c) how the knees extend and initiate a throwing-type action as the forward swing is completed.

Hip Action

Until recently, some teachers have questioned the involvement of the hips in hitting a serve or overhead and have therefore tended to overlook the importance of the hips. Teaching pros have always been aware of the legs and trunk because those segmental movements are obvious. However, contemporary knowledge now dictates that hip rotation may be the most crucial component in the difference between a great serve or overhead and a mediocre one. The hips are the area of the body where a skilled player transfers the linear and angular momentum generated by the legs to the trunk. If the hips are not used sufficiently in the movement, the serve won't be very effective. This is why Boris Becker has such a great serve. He usually hits the ball on the way down from its peak height, but he produces a high racket head speed by the way he uses his legs and rotates his hips and trunk. Without the phenomenal timing of his hip rotation, even Boris Becker's serve might be only average instead of one of the world's best.

Trunk Rotation

Once force is transferred effectively to the hips and they reach their maximum rotation velocity, the trunk is rotated. The amount of trunk rotation varies from player to player. Some players can generate a great deal of angular velocity from very little trunk rotation, but most good servers and smashers use a large amount of trunk rotation. As McEnroe hits his serve, for example, his hips can be seen facing to the side and slightly behind the court (Figure 8.3). In coiling the body this way, an athlete is able to create a lot of angular momentum with the trunk. However, it is extremely difficult to employ this excessive trunk rotation efficiently and still be able to sequence the rest of the motion properly. If you're not used to this motion, you might hurt your back. Be aware that trunk rotation is a necessary link in the chain, but don't try to overpower your serve with a lot of trunk movement. Work into it naturally so you can slowly develop an efficient force transfer from the trunk to the upper limb.

Upper Limb Motion

The next component in the system is rotation of the arm about the shoulder. In Figure 8.4, Stan Smith demonstrates some of the shoulder actions seen in serving and hitting a smash. By the time the trunk reaches its peak rotational velocity, the swinging arm should have gone through all of its preliminary actions and should be ready for the forward swing. (The arm motion during the backswing, by the way, should be used to help prepare the hips and trunk for their respective movements and to facilitate rhythm for the stroke.) When the arm is in its complete backswing position, it is externally rotated at the shoulder. As the forward swing takes place, the upper arm internally rotates at a high rate of speed.

Figure 8.3 Observe the large amount of body rotation John McEnroe employs to hit his powerful serve.

Elbow Action

Movement at the elbow occurs next as the player accelerates the racket head toward the point of impact. Figure 8.5 shows the elbow action necessary for a good serve. Two types of motion are involved at the elbow: extension from the flexed position attained in the backswing and pronation (turning outward) of the hand and forearm. Velocities for these two movements are extremely high and, combined with its fragile structure, cause the joint to be quite vulnerable to injury. Therefore, to develop this action, begin slowly until you get the rhythm of performing it correctly.

a   b

Figure 8.4   Notice the movement about the shoulder as Stan Smith swings forward toward ball contact in the serve and overhead smash.

The Wrist Snap

Some teaching professionals feel that pronation is the last movement prior to ball contact on the serve and overhead. These instructors say that a wrist snap does not really occur until after the ball is hit although we know that after impact much wrist flexion can be seen during the follow-through. Even though they feel that the snap doesn't happen prior to ball contact, these pros advocate that a tennis player think of using a wrist snap when developing the serve because it helps accelerate the racket head through impact.

Other tennis instructors argue, saying that wrist hyperextension actually takes place during the latter stages of the backswing and in the early phases of the forward swing. Then, as the racket head is accelerated toward impact, the hand flexes at the wrist until it is nearly straight relative to the forearm and actually snaps the racket through impact into the flexed position.

This debate has been predominant in many tennis circles in which players discuss techniques or teaching pros converse about instructional methods. Previously, little data have substantiated either opinion, but the following information will show what some of my studies have revealed.

Using three-dimensional cinematography and an electronic device for measuring angular change, my colleagues and I observed that players used wrist hyperextension as they began the forward swing. In addition, the wrist flexed from the hyperextended position through impact. It

a   b

c   d

Figure 8.5   Notice the upper limb action on this athlete's serve.

seems that the elbow extends and the wrist flexes from the "back-scratch" position at nearly the same time. To determine when each action takes place and how one contributes to the other is near to impossible.

From the results of this research one can assume with a great deal of confidence that the teaching cue of using a wrist snap is not only valid from the standpoint of helping a player develop the serve more readily but also because the wrist snap actually does occur before impact. I do not recommend, however, trying to consciously hyperextend and flex your wrist if you're trying to improve your serve. Just think of snapping the wrist and racket through impact and you'll naturally accomplish your goal.

Dr. Jack's Tennis Tips

When snapping your wrist, remember you must get the racket head through impact quickly. If the wrist leads the action, the racket will come through late and the ball will go long.

Why Do So Many Different Serving Techniques Exist?

When I discussed stroke form for the ground strokes, I said that due to the various grips available and the variety of swinging patterns you can use, it really doesn't matter what your strokes look like as long as you hit the ball correctly. For serving there are also a number of both efficient and inefficient methods.

Some serving methods have recently come under severe scrutiny by professional teachers and are the topics of interesting debates. Although research has provided few actual answers, I'll discuss the mechanics of some of these movements, hoping to enlighten you about what the techniques can and cannot offer. We will consider only three of the so-called efficient serving methods.

1. Allowing the hind foot to stay slightly behind and separate from the front foot in the serving motion versus allowing the hind foot to slide forward and take a position adjacent to the front foot
2. Landing first on the front foot versus landing on the hind foot following impact
3. Using a full backswing method versus a half-swing method

Service Footwork

The first technique deals with the footwork involved in serving. When you watch the pros play, you'll see two basic types of foot movement: The hind foot will stay separate from the front foot during the forward swing (Figure 8.6), or the hind foot will slide to a position adjacent to the front foot. During the discussion, remember how important the hips are in serving and that the orientation of the feet plays a large role in how the ground reaction force is transferred to and through the hips.

a   b

Figure 8.6   Notice how the hind foot stays separate from the front foot in the early part of the service motion, only to be brought forward once ball contact is accomplished.

The Platform Stance

When the feet are kept separate during the serve (usually about shoulder-width apart) forming a platform-type base of support, they provide a very stable base of support. This allows for an easy transfer of body momentum from the back foot to the front foot. The position of the back foot during the serving motion is the key to success using this technique. You've probably seen how McEnroe positions his feet when he begins his serving motion. His hind foot is placed quite far behind the front foot and he somewhat resembles a tightrope walker.

However, this is only a starting position. When McEnroe begins his forward motion, his back foot swings forward to a position adjacent to the front foot. This helps to generate a great deal of hip rotation. Many players, especially juniors who like to imitate McEnroe's strokes, have a problem using this method; such a player usually keeps the hind foot in a position where it blocks the hips from rotating effectively. If the hips are prevented from rotating, the serve will be poor. However, if the back foot is positioned so the hips are allowed to rotate or if the foot is swung forward, as McEnroe's is, then the hips can be used effectively.

The Pinpoint Stance

Often a skilled player will slide the hind foot forward during the serve so the feet form a small pinpoint-type base of support. The biggest problem for those who use this technique is maintaining body stability. One of the better performers can slide the hind foot forward, stay fairly stable, and still generate a great deal of force from the ground. Often a player who slides the hind foot forward will lose his or her balance, because a very small base of support is created when the hind foot is brought next to the front foot. With balance being of great importance, an efficient service motion is often difficult to achieve with this stance. This stance may be effective if stability doesn't seem to be a problem for a player, but as with the platform stance, the player must strive for adequate hip rotation. If the hind foot is incorrectly slid forward so it is behind the front foot or is held in a fixed position, hip rotation will not be allowed. That's why a skilled player using this technique usually slides the hind foot slightly forward of the front foot allowing the hips to be open slightly and capable of optimal rotation during the stroke.

Which Footwork Pattern Provides the Fastest Serve?

One unanswered question about these two methods of serving is this: Which one provides the server with the most force possible for hitting with high velocity? Is it the platform stance, in which the feet are approximately shoulder-width apart and the body well balanced, or is it the pinpoint stance, in which both feet are together allowing for the force from both legs to be applied to a very small area? The answer to this question is an interesting one. My colleagues and I studied the serving footwork techniques of several skilled players, using high-speed film and a force plate (a device that measures ground reaction force). One aspect of this study was to see which footwork action, platform (in which the feet stay apart) or pinpoint (in which the back foot slides forward near the front), provided more power on the serve.

We discovered that the pinpoint stance created more vertical ground reaction force, enabling the athlete to go a little higher in the air. This could provide a little more leverage for the serve, because the ball velocities for the pinpoint stance were slightly higher than those created by the platform stance. However, my suspicions were confirmed about balance. The centers of gravity of even these skilled players moved significantly when they used the pinpoint stance, whereas body control was much better when they used the platform stance. Thus, the decision is yours: Do you try to get more velocity by using the pinpoint stance, realizing that you must practice it a lot to develop sound body balance, or do you sacrifice a little velocity and go with the platform stance, which ensures more body control? Look at it this way: Boris Becker uses a platform stance and he hits a pretty good serve!

Which Foot Should You Land On?

No matter which method of service footwork you use, there is the problem of which foot comes through the motion the earliest to move into the court first. Some players allow their back feet to come around during the service motion and lead the way into the court, as demonstrated in Figure 8.7, whereas others let their back feet lag behind and lead the way into the court with the front foot (Figure 8.8).

a   b

c   d   e

Figure 8.7   Observe the difference when the player uses the crossover step and a half-swing serving motion. Notice that he brings the racket almost straight back from his starting position (a) to a position where it almost faces the back fence (b). In addition, observe that his hind foot is the first foot contacting the court following impact.

Figure 8.8 This tennis player demonstrates a noncrossover step and a wind-mill-type serving motion. Notice how he brings the racket downward so it is pointing toward the ground (b), and also be aware that his front foot is the first foot contacting the court (e).

Tennis authorities used to think that the hardest serves would be hit by those using the crossover step and coming into the court with the back foot first. The rationale behind this theory is that the back foot being brought through so quickly facilitates usage of the hips and trunk, because that leg helps the entire body rotate. This reasoning seems valid until you look at some of the better serves in the game today. Lendl and McEnroe, for example, do not use a crossover movement but head into the court with their front feet first. A second aspect of our serving foot-work study looked at the effects of the crossover step (in which the back foot comes into the court first) and the noncrossover step (in which the front foot comes into the court first). We found that the crossover step allowed a smoother and more efficient transfer of force through the body's linked system, whereas the noncrossover step enabled the player to get more vertical momentum but caused the action through the linked system to be very abrupt. The ball velocities from these two actions—high rotational momentum for the crossover and high vertical momentum for the noncrossover—were about the same, so no true benefit was derived relative to the final outcome.

Getting to the Net as Fast as Possible

The question now becomes this: If the two footwork motions do yield similar results, which allows its user to get into the net faster when playing a serve-and-volley game? The third and final part of our serving footwork research looked at this aspect of the serve. We found that the crossover technique allowed the server to get in only slightly quicker, but I should note that the problem could be one of inefficiency on the part of our subjects. Here's what we saw, however. The back foot in the noncrossover technique usually swung way out to the side (somewhat like McEnroe's does in Figure 8.3) making an awkward transition into a running stride for our players in the study. The crossover technique (Figure 8.7) allowed a much more efficient transition into the running stride. I would like to see more research in this area, however.

The Debate Over Arm Motion

The final controversial point to be discussed is the swinging motion in the serve. Although only a few basic methods exist that allow the player to hit a good serve, you would never guess this to be true while watching various players at your club or public park tennis courts. There almost seems to be a disease that causes players to develop idiosyncrasies once they learn the fundamental action of serving. Interestingly enough, this disease of developing unique idiosyncrasies is also seen in the pros. Roscoe Tanner had a quick rotary action that required incredibly accurate timing. Connors forms a hook with his wrist on the backswing that makes his serve conducive to high amounts of spin production. The list could go on indefinitely; however, we will discuss two basic methods commonly seen.

The Windmill Backswing

The most popular method of arm action in serving involves a full windmill-type swing (Figure 8.8). As the player takes a starting stance, the racket is lowered so that it is almost pointing toward the ground. Then the racket usually is brought up with an extended arm to a position of about shoulder height. From here the elbow flexes and the shoulder begins to rotate externally, allowing the racket to be positioned behind the back (some call this a backscratch position, but it really never reaches a true backscratch). At this point, the linked system of the body has generated its force from the ground and is transferring it to the hips and trunk. The shoulder continues to rotate externally as the trunk rotates forward, and at the approximate time when the trunk attains its maximum angular velocity, the shoulder accelerates its internal rotation to swing the racket toward the ball impact. As the racket head is further accelerated, the elbow extends, the forearm pronates (turns outward), and the wrist flexes to provide the racket with optimal impact velocity and to position it correctly for an effective ball contact.

The Half-Swing Service Motion

The second method of arm action is quite similar, except that instead of a full windmill-type swing the technique uses a half-swing motion (Figure 8.7). The racket, at the initiation of the swing, is not lowered so that it points toward the ground. Instead of dropping the racket head to that position, the swinging arm merely rotates out to the side and goes immediately to the position where the racket is held with an extended arm at approximately shoulder height. From this point, elements such as movements, the generation of force, and the transfer of that force to the racket are the same as with the windmill technique.

Dr. Jack's Tennis Tips

No matter how you take the racket back, try to keep your palm down as you bring the racket up toward the backscratch position. This helps to keep the arm and shoulder muscles relaxed, yet still prepares them for the serve explosion.

Differences Between the Two Backswings

Some authorities argue that a difference does exist between the two serving methods with regard to the amount of momentum produced during each swing. Many authorities state that the half-swing method doesn't permit the player to use his or her entire body to hit the serve in the most efficient manner. Others say that the main difference between the two serving types is rhythm. They feel that the half-swing technique doesn't allow the player to achieve a definite rhythm for timing the succession of events in the body's linked chain system properly.

Dr. Jack's Tennis Tips

The key to serving is rhythm. Regardless of the backswing you use, be sure you can comfortably generate a sense of rhythm.

It's difficult to say whether any difference in the generation of momentum is present between the two stroke patterns. From a purely biomechanical sense there should not be. However, there may be a definite variation of rhythm between the two strokes. For example, do you remember when you took serving lessons as a beginner? Your teacher probably told you that if you tossed the ball poorly you didn't have to swing at the ball (which is definitely how an improper toss should be handled). However, if you did go ahead and swing the racket, you could use the backswing to regulate the velocity of the entire movement. If you tossed the ball too high or if wind conditions prevented a normal swing, you could slightly slow and regulate your backswing to generate momentum effectively. The backswing in both serving methods can be regulated, but obviously the full-swing method allows more leeway for stroke accommodation. Regardless of that, however, it seems that the two service motions can be utilized effectively and their selection depends on personal preference.

Dr. Jack's Tennis Tips

Regardless of which backswing method you use, remember there is a purpose to the backswing—to prepare or coil your body for the explosion of serving. Thus, the backswing should be a relaxed motion performed with little muscular effort, but it should also be deliberate.

Why Do Some Players Serve and Hit Overheads Better Than Others?

As I said earlier, serving and hitting an overhead are both similar to an overhand throw in baseball (Figure 8.9). In fact, many sport scientists have shown that an effective throwing action is an absolute necessity in a championship serve or overhead, which is probably why some players have better serves than others. Good servers simply use a more efficient throwing motion, which causes the players to utilize the linked system most effectively. Therefore, let's see where some athletes go wrong in their throwing action.

Figure 8.9 Compare the actions of these athletes as they hit a serve (a), hit an overhead smash (b), and throw with an overhand motion (c). Similar body actions occur for each maneuver.

As you are aware, the primary source of power on a serve and overhead is the ground. The generated force is transferred through the legs to the hips and on to the trunk and upper limb. If a problem exists in the force transmission between any of these key body parts, the serve won't be effective. The one body segment that contributes to most service difficulties is the hips. Many performers don't employ the hips very well on the serve or overhead.

Surprisingly, many competitors, when describing their own service forms, feel that their bodies become long levers stretched out over the baseline at impact. It's not unusual to hear them say something like this: "I look just like Boris Becker when I hit the ball." They really do feel their service motions resemble Becker's when in fact they don't. Instead of using a proper throwing motion that involves hip and trunk rotation, such a player tends to flex the hips and force the trunk forward (much like Jimmy Connors in Figure 8.10) to hit a hard serve. Interestingly enough, this action of serving resembles one of the developmental stages of a mature throwing pattern. An analysis of the stages of developing an overhand throw may help you if your serve isn't as effective as you like.

Developing a Sound Throwing Action

When an individual (particularly a child) first learns to throw, he or she utilizes only arm movement to propel the ball. Realizing sooner or later that this motion alone won't propel the ball very far, and also by modeling better throwers, the individual will adopt a throwing pattern that involves a forceful forward flexion of the trunk. Somewhere during this

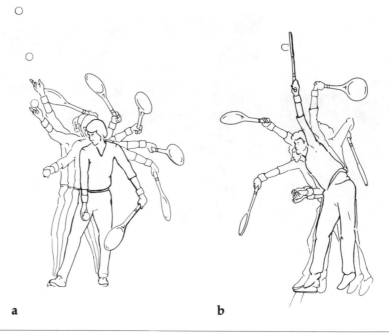

Figure 8.10   Notice how Jimmy Connors's service motion, depicted in (b), re-sembles that of any other player (a) except that his hind leg is prevented from rotating toward the court and his trunk is flexed forward forcefully at the hips.

process the novice thrower begins to step forward with the opposite foot as the transfer of linear momentum is developed. Finally the thrower acquires the proper skills necessary to coil the body segments, step forward, and uncoil the body parts as he or she learns to combine linear and angular momentum effectively.

Similar stages of body movement can be seen in the serve and over-head, the most predominant being the stage in which the trunk is force-fully flexed forward. A tennis player guilty of this can easily flex and extend the knees, but when the force nears its transfer to the hips the player can't coordinate the action. Instead of adequately rotating the hips, the player blocks the hips (prevents them from rotating) by keeping the hind leg fixed to the ground or in the air behind the body. Jimmy Connors is one player who has always performed this way. The only way Connors can hit a hard first serve is to forcefully flex his trunk forward. Players who use a technique such as Connors uses often can hit a fairly hard serve, but it's still not as good as it could be if the linked system were properly coordinated. To see if this applies to you, have your serve and overhead videotaped and watch the replay in slow motion. If your hips stick out backward toward the fence and your body is bent a great deal (a slight bend is all right), you may want to work on your overhand throwing action and apply the motion to your strokes.

The Service Hitch

Some people can employ all their body segments correctly but have such poor timing that they have a delay, or hitch, in their service motion. This hitch can occur at any point in the serve but occurs most often when the racket gets near the backscratch position (Figure 8.11). Several things may cause a hitch in a service motion, but the most common is poor timing between the tossing action of the ball and the swing of the racket. Often a player uses a very high toss and a quick backswing motion, so that by the time the racket is ready for the forward swing, the ball still isn't near the position of impact. Therefore, a delay in the swinging action must occur. This delay has more significance than merely slowing down the entire movement.

Figure 8.11   This is the position where the majority of service hitches occur.

Remember why the backswing is used? First, it sets the body by coiling the hips and trunk backward in preparation for the forward swing. Second, it helps a player to establish a rhythm for gaining momentum into the stroke and readying the shoulder and elbow joints for the upward and forward acceleration of the racket. For these reasons a hitch in the serve severely reduces the effectiveness of a service motion. In fact, the inefficiency of movement is so great that the player using this motion may as well begin the service motion at the location of the hitch rather than go through the other preparatory movements. The preliminary actions in the backswing become useless because of the way the hitch cuts down the generation of momentum. However, when you start a service motion from a backscratch position it is highly improbable that the service velocity will be as great.

Jumping Into the Serve

As skilled tennis players attempt to hit high-velocity serves, they often come off the ground during the motion. Some authorities say that a good server actually jumps into the serve (Figure 8.12). In fact, some teaching pros have analyzed slow-motion films detailing the service motions of highly skilled players at world championship serving contests. These researchers report that players who hit the fastest serves all jumped off the court. Frequently, the higher the jump, the faster the serve. However, it is extremely doubtful that the players actually jumped into the serves, especially to reach any particular height at which a peak racket velocity might be met. To attempt a purposeful and forceful upward jump when serving would require a unique amount of coordination and inhibit the tennis player's attempt to hit an effective serve. Therefore, we should not consider the leaping action seen during the serves of many

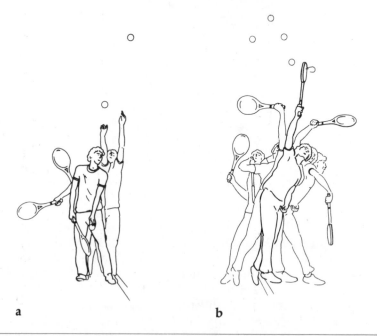

a   b

Figure 8.12   Notice how the player is off the ground during his service motion (b). Be aware that this is not a forceful jump; he is actually pulling his body off the ground due to the thrusting and throwing action.

world-class competitors as a necessity for hitting a good serve. These players, you see, generate so much momentum (both linear and angular) that the jumping action is the result of all the force created to hit a hard serve. If any of those players consciously jumped into their serves, the results would likely be poor.

Use of the Opposite Arm

No matter how much force is acquired from the ground and transferred through the body, one very important maneuver takes place to transmit a final thrust of force to accelerate the upper limb. When watching the next pro match on television, watch a player's opposite arm action during the serve or overhead.

The nonswinging arm never moves completely around to the side during the motion, but the elbow travels to the side and the forearm suddenly tucks in front and quickly positions itself across the lower chest wall (Figure 8.13). This motion contradicts some teaching techniques because it happens so fast that few people ever see it. Some teaching professionals make the mistake of teaching what they think happens, not what actually happens. Why does this motion take place? Recall what it was like in the high school locker room when you flipped someone with

a   b

Figure 8.13 Notice how the opposite arm follows the trunk around (a) and suddenly tucks in front of the trunk across the chest wall (b) during the service motion. This acts as a braking mechanism to decelerate the trunk rotation, allowing the upper limb to accelerate.

a towel or someone flipped you. How did the person flipping the towel make it pop so loudly? What happens is that the hand develops a high forward velocity and quickly pulls the towel along with it. The hand slows down and, as the towel passes by the hand, the hand forcefully accelerates backward. This pulls one end of the towel backward while the other end is still moving forward. The result is a loud snap, which means that if the towel is aimed correctly it can really inflict some pain. Realistically, the human body and its movements are not as simply explained as the motion of the towel. However, there are some similarities that can be applied to serving and to hitting a smash.

As the trunk attains a high velocity and the racket approaches the position from which it will be accelerated forward, the opposite arm comes across the front of the trunk. The opposite arm, acting as a brake, quickly decelerates the trunk and causes the upper limb to snap forward, somewhat like the towel. This elastic reaction provides the racket with a high velocity.

Should You Jump to Hit an Overhead Smash?

Many of the students I work with feel that they should jump into every overhead they hit. I'm not sure of the exact reason for this, unless they feel more powerful when airborne. I advise that you never jump unless you are forced to. When you hit an overhead with both feet on the ground as shown in Figure 8.14, your body is extremely stable. Once

a   b   c

Figure 8.14 Notice how this athlete maintains stability as he hits an overhead while he stays on the ground.

you are airborne, you have no control over your body's flight path. In essence, your body becomes a projectile. This means that you will follow a predetermined flight (however small it may be), causing a potential problem with balance and timing for the stroke.

One question I always receive is this: How is a ground reaction force involved when a player must jump to hit an overhead smash? A ground reaction force definitely does play a role in the jump overhead. When the athlete realizes he or she must leave the ground to reach and effectively hit an overhead smash (Figure 8.15), the athlete must first turn the body sideways to the net (somewhat like the initial serving stance). When the ball nears the player, the knee of the back leg flexes and extends forcefully, pushing the athlete off the ground. The extension of the back leg initiates a ground reaction force that is transferred to the hips and trunk just before the athlete leaves the ground. Some of the force generated from the ground is lost when the athlete leaps off the court, but enough remains and is transferred to the upper limb, allowing for a high racket velocity.

Figure 8.15 Notice in the overhead demonstration how to make your body a long lever and to use good body rotation when hitting a jump overhead.

Remember several things about a jump overhead before attempting one. First, once you leave the ground you have absolutely no control over the trajectory your body will follow until it reaches the court again. Therefore, stability in hitting a jump overhead is a necessity. You must maintain good control over the various body parts involved so that once you are airborne you can swing the racket efficiently. Second, because upper body control is so important, don't try to hit a jump overhead with high velocity. In slowing down your stroke a bit you will optimize your shot control. In my opinion, shot control is much more important than stroke velocity when you develop your jump overhead. Third, don't try a jump overhead unless it is absolutely necessary. When your feet maintain contact with the court surface you are in the most stable position, which not only facilitates shot control but allows you to develop greater velocity on the stroke.

Hitting With Control

The production of racket head speed is only one part of hitting an effective serve or overhead. The second part is control. Many players feel that because their rackets are so high above the net at ball contact, they must hit downward to keep the ball in play. They don't realize that even the most skilled tennis players have difficulty hitting downward and keeping the ball in play. In fact, it is a fairly well-accepted fact that a player must have a reach of nearly 11 feet with the racket and hit a flat serve at almost 100 miles per hour just to hit downward 3 degrees from the horizontal. Gravity and wind resistance have a tremendous effect on a flying object (like a tennis ball) once it has been struck. That's why most players who hit downward end up putting their serves and overheads into the net. The downward descent of the ball, combined with the effects of gravity, causes the ball to end up in the net. For this reason most good servers hit the ball straight out or slightly upward from the racket face even when hitting very high-velocity serves.

Dr. Jack's Tennis Tips

- To ensure net clearance on the serve, imagine hitting three balls in a row straight out from the racket. The first ball is your actual ball to be served, but pretend there are two more balls to be hit. Done properly, the ball will leave the racket at a 90° angle and you can let gravity work for you.
- If you're continually hitting long, try tossing the ball a couple of inches farther toward the net. Don't hit down but continue trying to hit three balls in a row straight out from the racket.

An overhead smash isn't necessary every time a ball is above your head; at times a high volley may be called for. This is especially true under two circumstances: when the ball simply isn't high enough to use the proper mechanics for an overhead, and when you haven't moved into the correct position under the ball. So don't try to overpower every high ball. Sometimes you must volley the ball deep and wait for your next chance at a smash.

The Second Serve

It has been said that a tennis player is only as good as his or her second serve. This makes a lot of sense if you consider that the opponent is usually expecting a high-velocity ball on the first serve. When you miss it, your opponent gains a big psychological advantage awaiting your second serve, which obviously won't be as hard. Therefore, it's necessary for any tournament player to not only work on achieving a high level of consistency in the first serve (approximately 70 to 75 percent during competition) but also to develop an effective second serve (95 percent during competition).

The racket head velocity is often faster during the second serve than during a first serve. However, the key point in hitting a good second serve is that the ball must have a great deal of spin (usually a combination of sidespin and topspin) to control its flight. This means that the racket must not only provide the ball with a great deal of forward impetus (although not as much as for a first serve) but must also quickly brush the back side of the ball to give it rotation. Therefore, the racket movement on a second serve doesn't move forward as quickly as a first serve, but because of the much faster vertical movement required for spin production, the overall racket velocity is often higher.

To develop a penetrating second serve you must attempt to hit the ball with at least three-fourths of the speed of your first serve. As you hit the second serve try to place some amount of topspin on the ball (it is difficult to hit pure topspin on a serve but a combination of topspin and sidespin should not be too difficult). Try to brush the ball from bottom to top in much the same way you hit a topspin ground stroke. The competitor in Figure 8.16 demonstrates how a good second serve should be hit. You can compare this motion with his first serve. Be aware that in Figure 8.16 his ball toss is not as far in toward the court and that the ball is also located more above his head at impact than it is for his first serve. This type of ball toss facilitates the necessary spin production. When you

a   b

c   d   e

Figure 8.16   This athlete illustrates how to hit an effective second serve. The goal of a good second serve is to hit the ball deep into the opponent's service court and with enough spin to maximize control.

practice this action, be sure to work on ball velocity, spin production, and depth into the service box. A short second serve (any serve in the front half of your opponent's service box) allows your opponent to step in and aggressively hit the return.

Dr. Jack's Tennis Tips

When trying to spin the second serve, let your wrist snap. Don't try to pronate excessively. Your elbow and shoulder rely on the pronating action as a follow-through mechanism to decelerate after impact. If you try to force the pronation, there is no follow-through and tendinitis could result.

NET RESULTS

It should now be obvious why the serve and overhead are among the most important strokes in tennis. With the number of people playing and the different methods of hitting the ball, it is no wonder players can be confused about the correct method of serving or hitting an overhead. It is essential to understand that the force generated in hitting an effective serve and overhead must come from the ground and that the force must be efficiently transferred through the body to the racket. In addition, once that force is transferred to the upper limb, it is important to concentrate on snapping the wrist through impact. Controversy about these strokes has existed for years, and I hope this chapter clarifies some issues for you.

Although much information is available about how the human body hits a serve and overhead, the only way to excel is to receive the proper instruction and to practice the method you are taught. Many people feel they perform the serve and overhead in an optimum manner—until they see themselves on videotape. When that occurs the reaction is usually, "Is that me?" Therefore, no matter how good you consider your serve or overhead, you may want to have a knowledgeable teaching pro critique these strokes.

C H A P T E R 9

It's a Game of
Continual Dire Emergencies

Peter Burwash, a renowned tennis instructor, has used the word *emergency* when speaking of the game of tennis. One of Peter's favorite stories is of the time he competed against Arthur Ashe in a tournament in the late 1960s. Instead of being on the offensive, as any skilled player would like to be, Peter found himself in a state of continual emergency. Ashe easily had Burwash running from side to side and from front court to back court. The interesting thing is that almost any tennis player has run into this situation, playing someone who seems to be in total control of the match. In fact, you never know what's going to happen next in any tennis match! With every movement of the opponent, you have to make adjustments in your own strategy and court position.

A mark of a great player is not only the ability to hit various spins, low hard drives, and soft looping moonballs, but the ability to receive each of these shots and counter the opponent's move. In that light, tennis is much like boxing, in which you have to take the offensive when you can but also must be able to counterpunch when you have to. With that in mind, we need to examine some of the emergencies you might encounter in match play and discuss how you can most efficiently react to each.

The Return of the Serve

At the initiation of every point in a match, a player is immediately placed in an emergency as he or she must return the serve. Not having any idea how the opponent will hit the serve, an athlete must be prepared to react to its placement and velocity. You never know if the opponent will swing you wide with a heavy slice, blast a ball right at you, or hit a kick serve to the middle. Therefore, to hit an effective return you must be able to read the velocity of the opponent's serve and the type of ball spin it has. You can refer to the chapters on the serve and ball spin to help you with this aspect, but we should discuss why some players make service return mistakes and how you can improve your own return of serve.

Ball Contact

Although most tournament competitors have extremely good eye–racket coordination, they often don't hit their service returns very well. Obviously, this may have something to do with how well the opponent serves, but it's not unusual to see poor returns of poor serves. The main reason is that when hitting returns many players don't have their rackets properly positioned at impact. Other players hold their rackets in the correct position but have little force behind their returns. In all of these cases, the athlete lets the ball play off the racket instead of letting the racket play the ball.

To hit an offensive return of serve you must attack the ball (Figure 9.1). This is true regardless of whether the return you wish to hit is a hard drive or a soft underspin return. If you don't think of returning aggressively, you're likely to mistime your swing and hit the ball poorly. A few coaching cues I've used in the past may help you achieve an offensive return.

First, watch how the opponent stands when preparing to serve. If he or she lines up in an open stance, a slice serve is a strong possibility. If a closed stance is assumed, the opponent may hit a kick serve. Be aware, however, that the more skilled a player, the better he or she can disguise these shots, so this strategy only works on less skilled players.

The next point is timing your first movement for hitting a return of serve. Assume your ready position near the baseline. As a general rule, stand about 3 to 4 feet behind the baseline if the opponent has a hard

a   b

Figure 9.1   This is often how John McEnroe attacks his return of serve. Observe how his racket contacts the ball well in front of his body regardless of his body mechanics. Although many players have better body mechanics, their racket heads are late getting to the proper contact point.

serve and at the baseline if the serve is mediocre. As the opponent takes his or her backswing, concentrate intently on the ball. Once the opponent begins the forward swing, take a short, balanced hop forward, as the player demonstrates in Figure 9.2. It is important that you maintain total body control during this small hopping action; don't jump too much or move forward too quickly. The purpose of the hop is to obtain linear momentum in your return. Try to time the landing of the hop so that your feet hit the ground when the opponent contacts the ball. In this way, you gain linear momentum forward and set the lower limb muscles to move one way or the other.

Immediately upon recognizing which side of your body the ball is traveling toward, use the unit turn to take the racket back in a slightly shorter backswing than usual (Figure 9.2). The unit turn allows you to coil your body for the stroke, and the short backswing enables you to swing the racket forward quickly. This is the most crucial point in your return. Think of getting the racket to the impact point quickly—but don't lift up as you swing. If you're lazy at this point, the racket won't be oriented properly at contact. Finish your swing with a good follow-through and move to a court position that prepares you for your opponent's next shot.

a

b

c

d

Figure 9.2 This athlete uses the forward balanced hop to return serve. His shoulder stays level throughout the movement.

Dr. Jack's Tennis Tips

As you use the balanced hop, don't go airborne too much and don't get caught going too far into the court. For example, if you are 3 feet inside the baseline on your return and the opponent hits his or her shot deep crosscourt, you're in trouble.

Types of Service Returns

There are basically two types of returns (besides the lob): a deep drive in which you hit and stay near your own baseline, and a shot hit short into the opponent's court. Either can be hit flat, with topspin, or with underspin. The purpose of a deep drive can be to keep the opponent on the defensive behind his or her baseline, to pull the opponent out of position by hitting crosscourt, or to go for a clean winner. You can use the short return to bring a baseliner to the net, to hit at the feet of a serve and volleyer, or to go for an outright winner by angling the ball crosscourt. Remember that you can follow either type of return to the net if you can take the offensive more readily against your opponent. One method of practicing service returns is to have your practice partner stand at his or her service line and hit serves into various parts of your service box. Have your partner vary speeds and spins to simulate first and second serves so you learn to react, move, and hit effective returns quickly.

Dr. Jack's Tennis Tips

When returning a serve, you can return to the three-word phrase used earlier in the book—ready, read, react! Be sure to keep your shoulders in control and avoid pulling out of the shot.

Must You Always Hit a Backhand?

Once the return is in play and the point is in progress, many players find themselves struggling as their opponents continually attack their backhands. Besides working to improve their backhands, these players should always bear in mind there will be times when the opponent won't hit a penetrating drive to the backhand side of the court. For whatever the reason, he or she will occasionally hit a soft floater or lob. If this happens to you, you don't have to hit a backhand.

Whenever you get the chance, feel free to run around your backhand and return the ball with a forehand (Figure 9.3). Not only will this make you a more offensive player, it will make your opponent think twice about hitting a soft shot to your backhand.

If the opponent hits a high lob to your backhand, you have two alternatives: run around your backhand and hit a conventional overhead smash, or hit a backhand overhead. You should use the same stroke mechanics as described in chapter 8 for the conventional overhead. The only difference is that quick lateral footwork is necessary to run around your backhand.

Figure 9.3   Observe how this athlete handles a softly hit ball to his backhand side. He quickly maneuvers around the ball so he can hit an aggressive forehand drive.

When you hit a backhand overhead, timing is of extreme importance. You must turn your body sideways to the net (Figure 9.4), internally rotate your upper limb so the racket is placed over your shoulder, step toward the net or jump (whichever is required by the shot), and externally rotate the arm to hit the ball straight out from the racket head.

Because this is naturally a weak stroking movement, the skilled player will practice it in order to enhance timing and control and to help make it a forceful shot. If you practice this shot be sure to work on control first. You should be able to direct the ball down the line as well as crosscourt. Once control is properly developed you can work on timing to hit a powerful shot.

a   b   c

Figure 9.4 This tennis player demonstrates the mechanics of hitting a backhand overhead when forced to leap in the air for the smash.

Dr. Jack's Tennis Tips

You should practice running around your backhand. Done correctly, it is devastating to almost any opponent. Just stay in control of your body and try to have your body's momentum moving into the court, not toward the sideline.

The Approach Shot

Unless you're the type of player who sets up camp at the baseline during a point, you need to be aware of how to get to the net most effectively. One way is to serve and volley, but another (and very important) maneuver is to hit an approach shot and go to the net. When the opponent hits a ball near your service line, it usually acts as your admission ticket to the net. But here is where many players run into problems. They prepare to hit the approach, but because of improper mechanics they make errors and lose points.

A player may continue to lose points by trying to approach the net in any way possible, or the player may pitch a tent at the baseline and leave only when the opponent hits very short into the court. Immediately upon hitting the return of the short ball, such a player retreats to the baseline sanctuary. We discussed in chapter 7 why it's so important to go to the net, so now let's talk about how to get there.

Anytime your opponent hits a ball short into your court (short refers to anything near the service line or closer to the net), it can serve as your personal invitation to the net. All you need to do is hit an approach shot and follow it to a strategic net position where you can take the offensive. Although many players realize the value of going to the net, they have difficulty doing so because they have poor approach shots. However, the problem may lie not in the approach shot itself but in how a player reacts to the opponent's stroke and moves to hit the approach shot.

Preparing for Your Approach Shot

Before describing the mechanics of an approach shot, I'll discuss two extremely important factors. First, you should always be aware of how the ball comes off the opponent's racket. During practice watch your partner's strokes carefully, and as a ball is hit try to immediately recognize where it is going, how hard it is hit, and what type of spin it has. This will help you get a good jump on a short shot so you can approach the net. Second, you should never let the ball drop too low before hitting your approach shot. The lower the ball is the more upward you must hit it to clear the net. The ideal point of contact is between waist and shoulder height, but if the ball doesn't bounce that high try to hit it at the peak of its bounce. Be sure your body is under control as you run toward the ball.

Movement Into Your Approach Shot

Traditional teaching advised that you never hit an approach on the run because you aren't balanced and will lose control. This advice is now out of date. Although it's true that you don't want to sprint into the approach shot, you can move through it and still be in control of your body. The most stable position in which to hit the approach shot is a standstill, but that position slows you in getting to the net, and a step or two closer to the net can be crucial. Therefore, many teachers currently advise students to "glide through the stroke." As shown by the athlete in Figure 9.5, keeping the body a bit lower than usual to maintain stability and turning slightly sideways allow a player to stride into the shot and hit deep, effective approaches. The sideways turn of the body will be greater for the backhand (especially the one-handed backhand) because of the orientation of the racket arm to the body. That's why you may see a player crisscrossing his or her steps to hit a one-handed backhand approach shot. This allows the player to turn the body sideways to the net yet permits gliding (via the crisscross steps) through the shot. This footwork is usually not seen for the forehand because the orientation of the racket arm to the body doesn't mandate the side turn. A player will usually turn slightly sideways to facilitate the forehand swing, but the crisscross stepping will not be as obvious.

a   b   c

Figure 9.5   Here you can see the footwork and stroking pattern necessary to hit a backhand approach shot. Following contact with the ball (c), the athlete continues to move through the shot toward the net.

Regardless of how far sideways you turn to hit the approach shot or how you choose to glide through the shot, the largest problem in body movement occurs in the middle of the stroke. Most players, as they hit approach shots, find themselves near the sideline of the court, because few of the opponent's shots will be hit to the middle. Realizing they are not in the middle of the court, they feel extreme urgency to recover from the approach shot and quickly get to midcourt. The problem is that they do it too soon. Many players move to midcourt before they ever hit the ball (Figure 9.6). They pull away from the approach shot too soon, causing their bodies to become unstable and resulting in errant strokes. The body must stay into the approach shot at least until the ball is hit. As a cue, I tell the players I work with to mentally draw a straight line between their shoulders. As they prepare to hit backhand approach shots, I ask them to keep that line directed toward the point of impact until they hit the ball. Once contact occurs, the player can move into position for the opponent's return. There is usually plenty of time to attain an advantageous position for your next shot.

Figure 9.6   This tennis player shows the wrong way to hit an approach shot. Observe how his body is already moving toward the center of the court as he hits the ball.

Topspin or Underspin on Your Approach Shot?

The preceding discussion and photographs involve approach shots hit with underspin. A controversy exists among many athletes as to whether a player should hit an approach shot with topspin or underspin. Some authorities prefer all topspin approaches, others advocate hitting all underspin approach shots, and still another group favors hitting approach shots above the net with topspin and those below the net with underspin. Wherever you stand on this issue, consider a few biomechanical facts. First, remember that topspin can only be hit with low-to-high acceleration of the racket head and that balls below the top of the net will most likely have to be hit with a slightly opened racket face to propel the ball upward to clear the net. Therefore, when you attempt to hit a topspin approach shot on a ball below the net you may have your work cut out for you. First, the racket face must be slightly open, which by itself creates a huge problem because the topspin approach of the racket head may cause the ball to go long. This factor, combined with the fact that you must get below the ball to create topspin when it is already below net level and closer to the net than usual, makes a topspin approach shot in this situation quite difficult even for advanced competitors. In addition, the topspin approach shot often causes you to lift your body excessively while trying to accelerate the racket head upward, creating even more problems for the stroke.

An advantage of the topspin in approach is that it can be hit with a great deal of velocity, especially from net height or above. The problem here is that if not enough topspin is placed on the ball it might travel long and if too much spin is placed on the ball it may bounce too short in the court to be effective. The argument in favor of topspin, of course, is that even if the ball does land short in the court, it will jump off the court and cause problems for the opponent trying to hit a good passing shot.

Underspin can also be used to cause the ball to jump off the court, but in a different way. Hit with a low trajectory, the underspin approach shot will skid, stay low, and force the opponent to hit up on the passing shot. This skidding action of the underspin approach is one of the reasons I prefer teaching this shot. The naturally beveled racket face required to hit underspin, combined with the necessary high-to-low motion, allows you to hit the underspin approach when the ball is in any position on the court. It usually cannot be hit with the high velocity used with topspin because of an underspin shot's tendency to float, but it can be hit as a low, deep drive that lowers the opponent's chances of hitting an easy winner. The biggest disadvantage of the underspin approach shot is that if you hit the ball lazily and it has a higher than normal trajectory the ball will sit up, allowing your opponent a great opportunity for an offensive shot and creating a new tennis emergency for you. See Table 9.1 for a comparison of the two approaches.

Table 9.1   Advantages and Disadvantages of Topspin and Underspin Approach Shots

Concern	Topspin	Underspin
Control	Can be difficult due to your forward movement and the vertical acceleration of the racket.	Usually is enhanced because racket speed doesn't have to be as high.
Velocity	Usually is very high.	Can be high but usually is not as high as with a topspin shot.
Depth	Can be achieved, but remember that topspin forces the ball downward, which may cause it to be short in the court.	Is easier to achieve, because underspin tends to keep the ball in the air longer, which allows the shot to be hit deeper with more ease.
Bounce	Is fast, but high.	Is slower, but lower (if ball approaches the court at less than 45°).
Low balls	Can be difficult to get up over the net and down into the court.	Are easy to hit over the net and deep into the court.
High balls	Are easy to drive with topspin.	Are easy to slice with underspin.

Dr. Jack's Tennis Tips

When practicing your underspin approach shot, think of ''knifing'' the ball with a long follow-through. Work on low trajectories and depth into the court.

When the Opponent Is at the Net

Just as you work on hitting on the run and hitting effective approach shots, so does almost every opponent you'll ever face. Your opponent also knows how to get to the net effectively, presenting you with yet another emergency: getting the ball by the opponent.

When an opponent takes the net against you there are basically four things you can do:

1. Hit a passing shot down the line
2. Hit a passing shot crosscourt
3. Hit the ball right at the opponent, attempting to catch him or her off guard
4. Lob over the opponent's head

The Passing Shot

As you attempt to pass a net player, the obvious goal is to hit the ball so it clears the opponent's lateral reach. You must hit the ball hard enough so it can get by the person before he or she reaches it, but, just as important, it must be an accurate shot. When your opponent reaches the net you have little time to think about what must happen. Each passing shot you hit depends on the velocity and placement of your opponent's stroke and on the opponent's location relative to where you hit your passing shot. It takes a great deal of experience before a tennis player learns the proper stroke mechanics to use in various situations. I suggest that you actually practice your passing shots a lot. Have your practice partner volley at the net. Hit a couple of balls to either side of the court (not trying for a winner), and from here play out the point. You get to work on your passing shots, and if you're unsuccessful, your partner gets to practice hitting volley winners. You can even expand the drill so the player in the backcourt can lob also, which will make the practice more realistic. Just remember a few things about hitting a passing shot

1. You don't need to go for the line every time. If you aim a couple of feet inside the lines, you'll usually win the point but you'll also give yourself some margin for error.

2. Use your opponent as a target from which to hit away. By attempting to hit your shots around the opponent, you'll find your accuracy quickly improving.
3. Play the percentages on your passing shots, and don't try for extreme angles.

The Lob

The lob is another alternative you have when your opponent is at the net. In fact, the lob may be the most underrated shot in tennis. It can be used to change the pace of play during a point or to give you more time to recover to a strategic court position when you've been pulled out of court, but it is especially effective when the opponent is at the net. You can hit a defensive lob in order to move the opponent away from the net and into his or her backcourt, or you can hit an offensive lob with which you are actually going for a winner.

The defensive lob is usually hit with underspin (Figure 9.7), which allows you more control and will also give the ball a bit more lift. A beveled racket face is necessary while you use a high-to-low swinging motion. The goal is to give the ball a high trajectory, clearing the opponent's reach and hitting the ball deep into the opponent's court, forcing him or her away from the net.

a   b

Figure 9.7 The defensive lob must be hit with slight underspin. Observe the beveled racket face sending the ball upward.

The offensive lob, seen in Figure 9.8, can also be hit with underspin but is generally hit with topspin. The topspin causes the ball to have a looping trajectory as it clears the opponent's reach plus causes the ball to pick up its horizontal velocity after the bounce.

Although many people feel the topspin lob is extremely difficult to hit, it doesn't have to be. Good timing is required, but you should think of a topspin lob as a modified ground stroke. For example, try hitting your normal topspin ground stroke with a practice partner. As you get a rally going, work in increasing the net clearance of your topspin shots. You may have to slow down your shot a bit, but don't try to hit any more topspin. Work on increased net clearance until your shots go about 15 to 20 feet above the net. Once you have the feeling of this stroking movement, remember it, because you've just learned how to hit an effective topspin lob.

a   b   c

Figure 9.8   Here you can see how a tournament player hits an offensive lob with topspin. Observe the steep low-to-high motion of the racket head.

What to Do if Your Lob Is Short

One shortcoming of the lob is that if you hit it short your opponent will be able to reach it and hit an overhead. Many players, once they realize they have hit poor lobs, give up and let their opponents hit whatever they wish. However, you will very seldom see a great player give up in such an instance, especially during a big point. If a ball is hit short, the elite competitor will wait until the last second (usually just as the opponent prepares to swing at the ball) and then sprint toward one side of the court. Trying to second guess the opponent in these situations can have big payoffs because you can often obtain a great deal of psychological momentum by returning a ball the opponent assumed was a clear winner. Therefore, don't stay in the middle waiting for the opponent's shot when you send over what's called a "duck" ball. You must go one way or the other; at least you will have a chance to get your racket on the ball.

NET RESULTS

Interestingly enough, the better your skills become, the more emergencies you'll encounter. How well you react to each emergency and accommodate your own movements relative to the situation determines whether you will continue to excel.

Here's my advice to help you improve your emergency skills. First, always try to maintain body balance regardless of the shot you must hit. Second, be sure to play the percentages whenever possible. Know your limitations, go for shots you're capable of hitting, and avoid the extremes. If you don't own a shot, don't hit it!

Finally, be a flexible tennis player. You must not only be willing to adapt to different match play situations, but you must be able to react to your opponent's moves. This is a major step on the way to championship tennis.

Facts and Fallacies of the Game

Many myths are associated with tennis. I have discussed some of these commonly misconstrued topics, but this chapter is a summary of some of the hard-to-believe (or misunderstood) facts and the most often misused myths. These myths have been developed over the years by players who talk about what they think they see happen on the court. The problem is that the naked eye is not precise enough to see what actually happens between the ball and racket. Therefore, I have compiled these facts and fallacies after years of examining tennis performances with high-speed film, which can be stopped frame by frame and studied.

Facts

Fact #1. *The fewer body segments involved in a movement (within reason), the less chance for error.* Using enough of your body to generate an optimal amount of force is necessary, but maintaining control over a specific stroke is also important. Players at times exaggerate their movements, using many segmental actions in attempts to develop more force or disguise a shot. Let's examine the ball toss when serving, for example. By using all three joints of the upper limb (shoulder, elbow, and wrist) when tossing, you increase the number of body parts that must be used accurately. Having three joints in action decreases your chances of placing the ball in the exact position to hit the best serve, because a movement error could occur in any of the three joints. Instead you should toss the ball with the upper limb moving only at the shoulder, thereby maintaining fairly rigid elbow and wrist joints and increasing the likelihood of an accurate toss. Your first objective is to determine how much force is required and what body parts must be involved to toss the ball with accuracy.

Fact #2. *Force in tennis comes from both linear and angular momentum.* Regardless of the type of shot you attempt, your body uses both linear and angular momentum to produce force. When you step into a shot, you create momentum in the linear direction of the step. Angular momentum occurs from the rotation of your hips and trunk to bring the racket head into position. Even during serves and open-stance ground strokes you use both linear momentum and angular momentum. In the serve, your legs extend to produce a linear ground reaction force, transferring this momentum to angular momentum at the hips. For the open-stance ground stroke, force generated from the ground in a linear direction is transferred via your hips and trunk in the form of angular momentum. The more important of these two types of momentum is the angular momentum obtained from hip and trunk rotation, because it provides impetus to your upper limb.

Fact #3. *Most of the force in tennis comes from the ground.* We know that for every action there is an equal and opposite reaction. The initiation of force to effectively swing a racket must come from the ground reaction force and be transferred through your body's linked system of legs, hips, trunk, and upper limb. The only shot in tennis to which ground reaction force does not apply is the punch volley (drive volleys usually do require force from the ground). Ground strokes, serves, and overheads all require an optimum ground reaction force to generate racket speed.

Fact #4. *The one-handed and two-handed backhands have similar reaches.* Up until the late 1970s, tennis instructors felt that the one-handed backhand was the preferred stroke because of its ability to reach farther in stroke production. A 1978 study found very little difference in reach between the one-handed and two-handed backhand drives when the player is in the proper position to swing the racket. There are the obvious problems with extremely wide shots or low approach shots for the two-handed backhand, but players using a one-handed backhand had similar problems on very wide shots.

Few offensive ground strokes occur when you are stretched out, even with the one-handed backhand. By using the two-handed backhand you can learn defensive maneuvers to use with one hand when pulled wide. Consequently, limited reach is not a valid reason to avoid learning a two-handed backhand.

Fact #5. *Larger headed rackets have larger hitting zones and also absorb vibration better than older conventional rackets.* Recall the discussion on moment of inertia: There are two ways to increase a racket head's resistance to rotation in the hand. The first is to increase the radius of the racket head (make it larger); the second is to add small weights to the perimeter of the racket head. Both ways increase the resistance to rotation by creating a larger effective hitting zone. Also, both ways tend to reduce the amount of torque from off-center impacts.

Fact #6. *The racket face must be near vertical to achieve optimal impact.* In almost every shot attempted, the racket face, at contact, must be nearly perpendicular (within 5 degrees) to the flight of the ball. The only time the racket can sway farther from the vertical is when you attempt underspin. Then the racket can open more than 5 degrees (but not much more), because the racket head's action is from high to low. The high-to-low swing accommodates a slightly open racket face and usually keeps the ball in the court.

Fact #7. *Changing grips during the volley as a beginner facilitates skill acquisition.* Changing grips during the volley has been widely debated. The only study on this topic indicates that beginning tennis players taught to change grips from an eastern forehand to an eastern backhand acquired greater control of the volley than beginners taught to use only the continental grip. Some of the players taught to change grips when volleying later tried the continental grip, again, this seemed to help them improve more quickly. They were able to hit forehand and backhand volleys more readily without taking time for grip changes. These findings suggest that a beginner should learn the volley by using a grip change, then switch to the continental grip at a later date.

Fallacies

Fallacy #1. *You should keep your eye on the ball.* The fact is that you should track the ball when competing, which is as close as you can come to keeping your eyes on it. It has been scientifically shown that as the ball travels toward the player it becomes a blur at 5 to 6 feet away, and vision usually remains focused at that point 5 feet away. The better the player, the easier it is for him or her to utilize a mental motor program (or image) of a stroke, anticipating where the ball will be based on projectile motion.

This procedure is more difficult for intermediates, who usually have not yet developed proper motor programs. The risk in telling intermediates to keep their eyes on the ball is that they actually try to do it. Some rotate their heads to maintain eye contact as the ball approaches. If the ball becomes a blur near you, head rotation creates a useless imbalance. Also, if you develop the bad habit of head rotation, you will have a more difficult time constructing a proper motor program for stroke production. It is better to use the cue "concentrate on the ball," which will not prompt you to turn your head as you swing.

Fallacy #2. *Tennis is a game in which you should be mostly on your toes.* Do this only if you want to have sore calves! In all of my high-speed film work, I found that the majority of foot contact with the ground as a player runs is heel strike. This does not mean you should be on your heels when you play. In fact, your center of gravity should be slightly forward over the balls of your feet so you can explode to the ball more readily, but don't try to stay on your toes.

Fallacy #3. *You should keep the racket head above your wrist when volleying.* The intent of this teaching cue is to minimize the amount of joint freedom in a controlled stroke like volleying, because unnecessary joint activity in a stroke does increase the chance of a mistake. With your wrist held fairly rigid, you can produce effective and penetrating volleys. In its literal sense, however, this cue is incorrect. If the angle at the wrist is static, your upper limb and trunk actions can position the racket head in various locations relative to other body parts. The racket head can even be positioned below your wrist with the same wrist angle as when held above your wrist. Therefore, key your playing on the wrist angle and not necessarily on the racket head position.

Fallacy #4. *Hit down on your serve.* The height of the extended racket during a serve often gives a false impression of the necessary trajectory for a serve. As mentioned earlier, many players feel that they must hit down on the ball to keep it in the service court. However, computer simulation proves that you must have a reach of about 11 feet with the racket and hit the ball at approximately 120 miles per hour to be able to hit downward 3 degrees from the horizontal. As few tennis players meet these physical requirements, it is important that you let gravity work for you. It is much better to hit the ball straight out from the racket or even to hit up when serving. From another perspective, it is much easier to develop your serve by hitting the ball beyond the service line and then working on bringing it back in than it is to hit serves into the net and then work on getting them over.

Fallacy #5. *You should turn sideways to the net when hitting ground strokes.* Although it is necessary to rotate your shoulders to the side, it is not necessary to turn your whole body sideways to the net, which only serves to fix you in one position and limit flexibility. The open-stance forehand requires hip and trunk rotation to develop optimal angular momentum, and your feet must be positioned to allow necessary rotation when stepping into the shot, but seldom must your body be completely sideways to the net.

Fallacy #6. *Intentionally jumping when hitting ground strokes or serves automatically increases power.* Leaving the ground is common in serving and hitting hard ground strokes. In fact, it has been demonstrated that the higher an elite player is off the ground, the more effective the shot hit. However, a great player never intentionally jumps when hitting a ball; rather his or her body is actually pulled off the ground by the leg action and body rotation. Movement off the ground is all right when hitting the ball! The primary concern is not that you are off the ground but at what point during the stroke you are off the ground.

When elite players leave the ground just prior to hitting a ground stroke, all the force they generate is in the small body parts (the upper limbs). If you leave the ground when the force generated is in your hips and trunk, the law of action/reaction will take effect. For example, if you leave the ground when all the force is in the trunk, that force will travel back down through the hips and the subsequent stroke will be poor. If you leave the ground when the force is in the upper limb, there is still a reaction of your upper limb against the trunk (a small body part against a large one), but the loss in negligible. Trying to forcefully leave the ground during a ground stroke or serve is unnecessary, because it occurs naturally as optimal and forceful stroke development occurs.

Fallacy #7. *You should keep the ball on the strings as long as possible.* During a 1980 French Open match between Jimmy Connors and Stefan Edberg, television commentator Donald Dell described one of Connors's maneuvers as the ''best shot of the tournament.'' Connors had hit a crosscourt approach shot as he went to the net. Edberg lobbed over Connors on the forehand side (Jimmy's left) and followed his lob to the net. Connors ran back and hit an unbelievable winner past Edberg, which Dell described this way: ''Jimmy ran back, held it, waited for Edberg to commit himself, and then passed him.''

Such commentaries are common, and such phrases are also used in coaching. When coaches talk about holding the ball on the racket, they intend to assist the student in lengthening the hitting zone of a stroke. Considering the acceleration of the racket head and the velocity of the oncoming ball, there is little you can do to vary contact time. Besides, the longer a ball stays on the strings, the greater the chance for a mistake to occur (see chapter 2).

The phrase has become common probably because some athletes seem to control their strokes so well that they give the impression that the ball is held on the racket face, as Dell described. When you attempt to pass an opponent who is in an attacking position at the net, you want to wait until the opponent commits (by shifting center of gravity) and then hit the passing shot. Apparently rather than holding the ball on the strings you hold the backswing a bit longer. This lets the ball drop a little, thereby placing extreme time limitations on your opponent, who usually moves or leans in one direction or the other. Once detecting this directional commitment, you simply stroke the ball in the opposite direction.

Fallacy #8. *You should feel the ball on the strings.* When impact occurs on the racket face, the signal (or vibration) must travel through your racket, hand, forearm, upper arm, shoulder, and neck before arriving at your brain, a trip that takes about 50 milliseconds. As mentioned previously, the impact of the ball on the racket lasts between 3 and 8 milliseconds. The time lag between impact and the sensation of impact is at least 10 times longer than the impact itself. Consequently, by the time you feel the ball hit the racket, the ball is about 1 to 2 feet off the strings on its way back across the net.

Some players have used this cue ("feel the ball on the strings") to try to change their movement patterns at the last second to hit better shots. This is not only impossible to do, it is also harmful to even try; it will only hurt your chance of improvement. Once you initiate the forward swing and the racket accelerates, you should not try to change the intent of the stroke. Any change should occur prior to the initiation of the stroke.

The one time when the cue "feel the ball on the strings" can be effective is when you receive feedback about what was wrong with a certain shot. If you are encouraged by your coach to note how a bad shot feels, you may be able to avoid that feeling in future shots. Used this way, this cue could be a helpful coaching tool.

Fallacy #9. *You should run with the racket back.* The human body is not designed to run with an arm extended or to run while holding a long implement weighing several ounces. If your goal is to sprint into position, you must learn to use your arms in the normal pumping action associated with sprinting. This facilitates balance and allows you to generate the proper rhythm for quick sprinting actions. When you hold the racket back in position for the swing, balance is precarious.

Because running with the racket is an advanced skill, however, beginners and intermediates may be better off moving toward a shot with their rackets held back. Although they will not be able to run their fastest, early racket preparation will enhance stroke accuracy. When a less skilled player tries to run toward a ball and swing, timing is usually poor. If you fall in this skill category, this cue may be effective in helping you produce an optimal combination of movement and stroke. As you develop, however, you must learn to move with the arm and racket held in a way that allows for optimal speed and balance.

Fallacy #10. *You should bevel the racket horizontally to hit underspin.* Although the racket should be slightly open to hit an underspin drive, avoid opening the racket face too much. True, the best underspin players have their rackets extremely open in the backswing and also in the follow-through, giving the impression that the racket is extremely open on contact. What actually occurs is that the racket is open in the backswing because of the internal structure of the shoulder. As the forward swing is initiated and impact is near, the racket actually becomes nearly vertical. Then, to maximize the follow-through, the shoulder again rotates giving the impression of the open racket face.

Fallacy #11. *You should roll the racket head to produce topspin.* Although some players seem to actually roll over the ball to hit topspin (like everyone used to think about Bjorn Borg), it has been repeatedly demonstrated that this does not occur. The only way to produce topspin is to initiate the forward swing below the impact point and brush the backside of the ball in an upward manner, completing the stroke with a high follow-through. The more vertical the swing, the more topspin can be applied. A rollover appears to occur because of the internal structure of the shoulder joint. As your arm comes across your trunk in the follow-through your shoulder rotates, giving the appearance of a rollover that is meant to maximize spin, but this rollover does not even begin until the ball is about 1 to 2 feet off your racket.

Fallacy #12. *You should roll the ball crosscourt or hit the ball early to go crosscourt.* This common instruction gives you the false impression that this is the only way to hit a ball crosscourt. When you hit with direction (down the line, to midcourt, or crosscourt), the position of the racket face determines where the ball goes. A ball does not have to be hit early or with heavy topspin to go crosscourt. You can actually go crosscourt with a ball that has gotten behind you simply by correctly positioning the racket face. The same holds true for the old teaching adage "hit late to go down the line." Because the orientation of the racket face determines the flight path of the ball, these instructions are only successful when they happen to result in correct racket position. Impact timing is not the determinant.

NET RESULTS

I hope you find this discussion of facts and fallacies useful. The discussion should help you understand the physical basis of these concepts and show you how to employ some of the less obvious ones in your own game. Now the job is to put the ideas in this book to practice and prepare yourself for tournament competition.

C H A P T E R   1   1

Are You Ready for Championship Tennis?

Now that you've been exposed to the effects of sport science on the game of tennis, with specific emphasis placed on improving your game, where do you go from here? Are you ready to go into competition implementing some of the things I've discussed? If you're not ready, how will you know when you are? Although the answers to these questions are difficult to determine, I'd like to summarize some of the major topics in the book and combine them with a few general coaching tips. As you read this chapter, always apply what is said to yourself and your game. In that way I think you'll be able to improve your game most efficiently.

Be in Control and
Let Your Racket Do the Work

When playing competitive tennis, many athletes become so intent on hitting high-velocity shots that they literally put their entire bodies into the stroke by jumping as they swing (Figure 11.1). Not only is this unnecessary, it's harmful to your game; when you use your entire body incorrectly (as when jumping into a stroke), loss of control will result. Therefore, I suggest that you think of driving only your tennis racket into the ball at impact. Remember that your racket is the only part that hits the ball while the rest of your body merely supplies the force. So, when you prepare to hit a powerful stroke, don't let your body go out of control, because it is your power supply. Instead, imagine your racket driving through the ball at impact.

Figure 11.1   Notice how Steffi Graf leaves the ground on this ground stroke. She actually pulls her body off the ground but does not consciously try to jump into the shot.

Make Things Happen During a Point

When people enter the competitive levels of tennis, they tend to become extremely tentative when playing points. They often go on the defensive and hope that their opponents will make mistakes. Be aware that you cannot wait for something to happen in championship tennis! Yes, a player can attain a certain level of success by staying at the baseline, retrieving all of the opponent's shots, and waiting for an error. However, to excel in the higher levels of tennis you must learn to make things happen—not wait for them to happen. You can do this by thinking aggressively and attacking the opponent's weaknesses when the opportunity arises. However, don't go overboard with aggression and allow your stroking actions to go out of control.

Hitting Shots You Own

In the heat of competition, many players attempt to hit low percentage shots that they later (when the points are over) realize they should never have tried. At the elite levels of tennis, the ability to judge shots that are within your capability and to hit accordingly is called being able to hit the shots that you own. For example, when you're in a certain position on the court, don't attempt to hit an extremely difficult shot, but try your best to play the percentages. In doing so you'll find yourself a great deal more successful than if you go for the outrageous shots that even the best players don't try.

Watch Out for Idiosyncrasies

When you analyze the game style of a pro, decide what the real performance attributes are and what causes the action to occur. You can learn a great deal from examining how a professional athlete executes a certain stroke or movement pattern (Figure 11.2), but you must look specifically at the total action, body part by body part.

Figure 11.2 Notice how this player employs the unit turn to prepare his body.

Know What Goes Into the Perfect Stroke

Remember that to hit an effective stroke, good footwork is required not only to move but to generate a ground reaction force. The force is then transferred through the hips and trunk to the upper limb, generating impetus for the racket. There is only one point in the entire motion when a stroke must be perfect: impact.

What matters is not how you look during the backswing or the follow-through but only how the racket hits the ball during the .003 to .008 seconds of impact. Some general statements hold true here. Although basic, they may help you.

1. If the ball goes too far upward off the racket face, the racket face was too open at impact.
2. If the ball travels into the net, the racket face was too closed at impact.
3. If the ball goes to the right (for a right-handed player), the racket head was angled in that direction.
4. If the ball travels to the left (for a right-handed player), the racket head was angled in that direction.
5. If a ball is hit weakly into the court where the opponent can take advantage of it, the stroke may as well be called an error. Remember, if you are to improve, you must have the correct racket head speed to control the point.
6. For the most effective impact, the racket face should be nearly vertical.

Use of a Teaching Pro and Visual Aids

Due to the ball velocities and time durations involved in some of the situations I've just mentioned, it's virtually impossible for you to determine where a problem might lie in your stroke production. That's where trained professional teachers and coaches can help you. They have learned how each body part interacts with one another and the contribution of each to the total performance. However, at times even a trained eye has difficulty in detecting a movement error. This is where various types of visual aids can be extremely helpful. Still pictures, film, and videotape can assist you and your instructor in analyzing how effective and efficient you are, because these media allow the high-speed action of a tennis stroke to be slowed so each body part can be specifically examined.

Only one problem exists with this approach: Some athletes are so intrigued by seeing themselves in slow motion and being able to effectively study their own games that they begin analyzing their strokes all the time. Sometimes this goes so far that they scrutinize their movements during match play, which can be seriously detrimental to performance. This phenomenon is called "paralysis by analysis." Therefore, use a coach and visual aids as you need them, but don't get so involved with the analysis that it affects how you play. In this way you will reach your potential in tournament competition in the most efficient manner.

Use an Effective Speed–Accuracy Trade-Off

As you improve your skills and become involved in more high-level competition, you must be able to interchange speed and accuracy at will. There will be times when it's desirable to hit a high-velocity shot, but the game of tennis is mostly a game of control. Seldom will you need to hit the ball as hard as you can. A well-placed shot with medium speed is often much more effective than a high-velocity, poorly placed stroke. More realistically, you need to vary velocities and ball spins to maintain optimal control and to prevent your opponent from becoming grooved to your strokes. As far as control goes, a few general playing tips may be helpful.

- If you must hit a ball from a corner of your court, a crosscourt shot allows you more court to hit toward (Figure 11.3).
- When you hit a crosscourt shot, the ball travels over the lowest part of the net (3 feet high in the middle versus 3 feet and 6 inches high at the sidelines).
- Your most effective strokes will usually be deep in the opponent's court.

All of this, however, depends on how well you react to the emergency created by your opponent's previous shot.

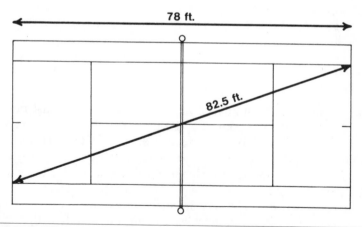

Figure 11.3 When you hit a ground stroke crosscourt, you have more court available to hit into; a bonus is that the net is lower at the middle than at the sideline.

Work on Adapting to Emergencies

Just as you try to dominate your opponent by varying your stroke production and placement, your opponent will try to do the same thing to you. That's why it's important that you not only develop effective footwork and strokes but also that you work on hitting effective returns of shots hit the same way. That is, you must practice returning low-bouncing balls, high-bouncing balls, wide shots, deep shots, short shots, and balls with different spins on both your forehand and backhand sides. You also need to practice a serve-and-volley strategy, and you must learn how to effectively hit an approach shot on a short ball. Once you get to the net, you must refine your low volley, high volley, touch volley, angled volley, and overhead smash. The list could continue, but you are probably aware of the areas on which you must work. Whatever your priorities are in practicing to achieve a well-rounded tennis game, remember that everything occurring on the court during the match is situational. The opponent's position in his or her court, your position in your court, and the shot your opponent hits are some of the factors that determine what shot you hit in return. And the only way to develop these areas is to practice them in a competitive setting like a practice match.

Goal Setting With Mechanics in Mind

Regardless of your current skill level, your goals for stroke production should involve the four concepts crucial to skill acquisition and competitive performance:

1. Control
2. Consistency
3. Depth
4. Power

The key point for almost any player is that power is the last phase of stroke development and control is the first. You must learn to control movement patterns to achieve optimal stroke production. This includes the ability to hit down the line, crosscourt, and to specific areas of the court. Control does not necessarily mean being able to hit a dime on the court, but you must work to achieve some measure of accuracy.

The second part of the stroke-production goal involves consistency. Once you attain control, you must learn to hit consistently with accuracy to various parts of the court. This requires you to maintain balance and properly use your body to enhance shot effectiveness. If you are at a lower skill level, try the inarguable strategy that the last player to hit the ball in the court wins the match. This sounds simple, but the more balls you keep in play, the more pressure you place on the opposition and the more confidence you gain. At higher skill levels you must combine control and consistency along with the third factor—depth.

Stroke depth is crucial to upper level tennis performance. If you can keep every shot within 5 feet of the baseline, then your opponent is kept behind the baseline where attack is difficult. Many athletes tend to forget the importance of depth and go directly to power. They hit very hard offensive strokes, but end up hitting into an area around the service line. Regardless of the force behind a shot, lack of depth allows the opponent to move in, using forward momentum to take the offensive during a point. At most skill levels it is much more effective to take some power off the ball and hit it deeper into the opponent's court. The more consistently deep your strokes, the more effectively you can take advantage of the opponent's court position and any other match situations.

The final factor in stroke development is power. To be able to hit with control, consistency, and depth is marvelous; adding the element of power puts you near world-class ability. Most players do not wait to develop the first three elements—they want to go immediately to powerful strokes. This is probably the biggest mistake they will ever make in their tennis careers.

As I have said, if you merely hit powerful strokes without control, consistency, or depth, you are asking for trouble. Never just hit powerful ground strokes or volleys. Instead, try to penetrate the opponent's court; gear your mentality to a goal of placement in the opponent's court, not to swinging hard. As soon as you start swinging hard, you disorganize the body's linked system and overwork your arm. Remember that although the upper limb contributes to the force of a stroke, it is above all a controlling mechanism, whereas the legs, hips, and trunk are the major force producers. Try to deliver solid, controlled shots that penetrate deeply into the opponent's court. Power will develop as a natural result of control, consistency, and depth.

Practicing Effectively

Practice doesn't make perfect; perfect practice makes perfect. I've seen many players practice several hours a day for years and still not achieve the levels they might have attained if they had practiced more effectively. Effective practice involves not only working with a good coach and being aware of your own stroke production but also having the right mental attitude during practice sessions.

Many athletes don't learn from their mistakes. It's almost as though they practice the same errors over and over. I suggest that as you practice you bear a few thoughts in mind

- Try not to make the same mistake twice (e.g., don't continually hit balls long, but rather use various forms of topspin combined with a slower velocity to gain confidence in the stroke and to regain your timing).
- Have a determined attitude when you practice, just as though you were in a match situation.
- Practice on all surfaces (hard court, clay, and grass) and in all situations (e.g., wind, bright sun, indoors, and outdoors, and so on) so you can accommodate your game whenever necessary.
- Conduct your drills to simulate all the emergencies that could present themselves during a match!
- Initially practice a new skill for about 5 minutes, then do something else before returning to the new skill for another 5 minutes. Try to practice the new skill 3-4 times per hour for a total of 15-20 minutes. You will learn the skill more effectively this way.
- Remember: It's the quality of practice that will make you better, not the quantity.

Don't Be Afraid to Put Yourself on the Line

There is only one basic reason you get nervous during a match: You are too concerned about whether you will win or lose. Face it; all of us who have competed in tennis have, at one time or another, choked. Did you ever wonder why you get so worked up over a match? Here's my analysis.

Tennis is a game that pits one on one, much like boxing. When you play poorly, you have no one else to blame. And the worse you play, the worse you feel. We tend to measure our self-esteem by the results of our matches, and we place little emphasis on how we play each specific point.

Unlike football, basketball, or soccer, there is no clock in tennis. When you have a lead, you can't play it safe and wait for time to run out. The game is full of stories about players who were up 6-0, 5-0, 40-love and yet lost. In fact, did you know you can lose 47 points in a row (6-0, 5-0, 40-love) and still win the match? As unlikely as that seems, you can't argue the beauty of the scoring system. You've never won the match until you've won the last point.

These are my recommendations for becoming a better tennis competitor.

1. *Make everything that happens on the court a challenge.* Use factors such as the wind or sun to your advantage. Above all, don't let them put you down.

2. *Manage mistakes positively.* If you make a mistake, respond to it by visualizing what the proper shot should look like; you can even break a smile. Whatever happens, stay positive about yourself.

3. *Control your emotions.* For 95 percent of the points a great competitor (e.g., Becker) plays, you cannot tell by the facial expression whether that player won or lost the point. Only 5 percent of the time does a great player show extremely positive (e.g., the Becker boogie) or extremely negative behavior. It's alright to clench your fist and say "Yes!" but just don't lose control.

4. *Prepare for each point with a game plan.* Before you ever step up to the line to serve or receive you should know what you'd like to do. Obviously, that's much more difficult on the return of serve because you must react to the opponent's serve, but you should still have an idea of what you want to do with the ball.

5. *Play one point at a time.* This is easy to do when you're behind because you know it's the only way you can get back into the match. However, you should also do it when you're ahead. Tennis is a game played one point at a time no matter what the score is or who your opponent is.

6. *When it's time to compete, it's not time to think about stroke mechanics.* If you deal with how you're hitting the ball, you won't compete at your best. In fact, you'll most likely experience paralysis through analysis. You can use practice matches to work on stroke mechanics in competition, but if the match you're playing is of importance, be a competitor and just get the job done.

If you want to learn more about competing and some of the issues behind the mental game, I suggest you consult the references at the end of the book.

Anticipating All the Possibilities

Anticipation in tennis deals with many facets of the game. One that I've already mentioned in this chapter is the emergency. As you play competitively, you will continually be placed in one emergency after another. Obviously, you must learn how to handle each predicament as it presents itself, and the only way to do this is to experience each one during match play. Practice sets and matches will help, but you need to become involved in sanctioned United States Tennis Association tournaments. Playing under the pressures of these tournaments is the only way you will become "match tough." To get a schedule of tennis tournaments held at the national, sectional, or district (regional) level, request the information from the United States Tennis Association, 1212 Avenue of the Americas, New York, NY, 10036.

Another part of the game that requires some type of anticipation is understanding what the opponent is capable of doing during a point. You can use the sport science information presented in this book to actually analyze your opponent's game; do this analysis during the warm-up and during the first few points of the match. As you warm up, for example, notice whether the opponent hits deep and with heavy spin. If not, perhaps you can attack by approaching the net on a short ball. When the warm-up is over, you should be able to generalize your opponent's capabilities; when the match begins you'll find out how correct you are. Your primary responsibility is to play your own game, but test the opponent when the situation arises. For instance, go to the net and see what happens. Don't be discouraged if you lose a point; the opponent may have hit a lucky shot. However, if you try something as a test of the opponent's capabilities in a certain situation and you lose several points doing it, you will need to change your strategy a bit. One possible change in strategy for the example I've mentioned may be for you to stay at your baseline and bring the opponent to the net. By now you may be aware of how important it is to be flexible with your strategy during a match. Sticking to one specific game plan could be your downfall. However, if it works, don't change it!

The final type of anticipation necessary in competition is knowing your opponent's shot capabilities during a point as he or she is located on various parts of the court. For example, when McEnroe hits a very soft looping forehand that barely clears the net and dips toward his opponent, who is located at the net, he often takes off running toward the net at the angle where he thinks the opponent will hit the ball. The television announcers say that McEnroe's anticipatory capabilities are phenomenal. However, consider what options the opponent has available to him when McEnroe hits a short topspin shot that barely clears the net. The only shot the opponent can hit is a short angled drop volley. Therefore, McEnroe anticipates how and where the opponent will hit the ball before his own shot even clears the net and starts running for that position on the court. In actuality, instead of anticipating what the opponent will do, McEnroe sets himself up by forcing the opponent to hit a certain shot.

You can also set up a point, but you must be able to answer many questions, such as the following.

- Can the opponent hit down the line on a wide shot?
- Does the opponent have good touch?
- Can I approach the net on his or her second serve?
- When I go to the net, will the opponent attempt to pass me on one particular side each time?
- Can the opponent lob well?

NET RESULTS

These are but a few of the things true championship players notice when a match is in its early stages. Obviously, they don't have to ask themselves each question during a match. Through years of tournament competition, they have learned to recognize when their opponents have trouble performing a certain stroke under specific conditions. You can acquire the same ability, but it may come to you more easily because you can employ your sport science background to make yourself a true championship player.

Glossary

acceleration—The ability to increase speed.

agility—The ability to change direction quickly, yet under control.

angular (rotational) momentum—A property of objects in motion that results from the object's resistance to rotation multiplied by its rotational velocity.

approach shot—The transition stroke that helps the player go from a position at the baseline to the net.

backhand overhead—A stroke often used to hit a high shot over the backhand side of the body.

backscratch position—The position where the racket is dropped behind the shoulder during the serve.

base of support—The area under the foot or feet.

bevelled (open) racket face—The position in which the upper edge of the racket face is slanted backward away from the vertical.

biomechanics—All of the mechanical forces at work within the body to create movement. External forces such as wind and gravity also affect biomechanical efficiency.

block—(1) Positioning the racket forward to just get the ball back in volleying or the serve return; (2) the hips' being prevented from rotating during a shot.

center of gravity—A point slightly above the center of the pelvic region about which all of a person's mass is distributed.

center of percussion—An extremely small point (similar to a sweet spot) usually located just below the geometric center of the racket face toward the throat on the racket face. If the center of percussion is impacted, the force to the hand is zero.

centrifugal force—The force that radiates outward from the center of a rotating object (as when the racket is pulled away from the body during a swing).

championship ball—A ball covered by less wool nap than an extra-duty ball; the championship ball feels slightly lighter at contact.

closed racket face—The position in which the upper edge of the racket face is slanted forward past the vertical.

closed stance—The stance used when the player steps across with the foot opposite the side where the ball will be hit.

coefficient of restitution—The index of elasticity of an object that describes how a body (e.g., a ball) will deform and regain its original shape during and after impact.

continental grip—The grip that situates the V between the thumb and forefinger of the swinging hand over the inside bevel of the racket handle.

coordination—The ability to properly place the body relative to the ball for each shot and to properly sequence the appropriate body parts into each shot.

crossover step—The footwork on the serve where the back foot enters the court first.

cross section—The thickness of a racket.

dishing—Moving the racket under and around the ball during a volley.

drive volley—A shot that is hit before the ball bounces by using a long stroke.

drop volley—A softly hit stroke that lands the ball very short in the opponent's court.

duck ball—A set-up shot, or one that floats with little speed.

dynamic balance—Overall body control in moving toward a ball and hitting the shot. See also *static balance*.

eastern backhand grip—The grip that situates the base knuckle of the swinging hand over the top flattened surface on the handle as the racket face is oriented vertically.

eastern forehand grip—The grip that situates the V between the thumb and forefinger of the swinging hand over the top flattened surface on the handle as the racket face is oriented vertically.

effectiveness—Velocity and depth of shots.

efficiency—Economy of motion.

extension—Increasing the angle between two body parts (e.g., straightening the knee).

external rotation—The position of the swinging shoulder in the serve and overhead when the upper limb is held up at 90° to the trunk with the elbow flexed and the hand located behind the head during the backswing.

extra-duty ball—A ball covered by more wool nap than a championship ball. The extra-duty ball is more durable.

flexion—Decreasing the angle between two body parts (e.g., bending the knee or elbow).

floater—A ball traveling with little velocity.

force plate—A piece of equipment that measures ground reaction force.

friction—The contact of opposing forces from two different surfaces (e.g., tennis shoes and the court).

gauge—A string's thickness.

ground reaction force—The force emitted from the ground as the body pushes against it.

ground stroke—A shot hit following the bounce of the ball (most often hit from near the baseline).

half-open stance—The stance in which a player sidesteps toward the ball but does not completely rotate the body in preparation for the shot.

half-volley—A stroke that contacts the ball immediately after it bounces off the court surface.

harmonic action—The type of vibration frequently seen in a racket following impact.

Har-Tru—An artificial clay known to be slow, implying that increased friction results between the court and ball, slowing the ball down after it hits the court.

heavy slice—A driving stroke that places great underspin on the ball.

heel counter—The area of the shoe's sole under the heel, which sometimes elevates the heel.

heel cup—The area of the shoe that surrounds the heel.

hitting zone—The sweet spot.

hyperextension—Extension of a joint beyond the straight position (e.g., when the hand bends backward at the wrist).

idiosyncrasy—A movement peculiar to an individual.

inside-out shot—A stroke that accelerates the racket from close to the body (inside) away to the outside (i.e., hitting a forehand from the left side of the court to the opposing corner).

internal rotation—The position of the swinging shoulder in the serve and overhead when the shoulder rotates to move the hand and racket forward toward impact.

kick serve—A serve that bounces high and opposite its flight path.

line of gravity—A line dropped straight down from the center of gravity.

linear momentum—A property of movement associated with the body (as a moving object), which is based on its mass multiplied by its velocity. This property can be transferred to the tennis ball to enhance its movement.

linked system (kinetic chain)—The successive integration of body segments to generate optimal force for a tennis stroke.

lob—A shot hit high into the air and deep into the opponent's court.

lunge—A long stride and stretch to return a shot.

midsized racket—A racket whose face size is around 90 square inches.

moment of inertia—An object's resistance to rotation.

momentum—A property of an object in motion equal to mass multiplied by velocity. Momentum causes an object at rest to resist motion, but once the object begins to move, momentum causes the object to keep moving, resisting the cessation of movement.

nap—The wool covering on a ball.

neutral position—A ready position in which no particular stance is assumed but the player is ready to move.

noncrossover step—The footwork pattern in serving in which the front foot is first to enter the court.

nonpressurized ball—A ball not in a vacuum-sealed container.

open stance—A stance used when the player steps toward the sideline with the foot located on the same side as the ball.

oscillation—The back-and-forth action of a racket following impact.

oversized racket—A racket whose face size is over 100 square inches.

passing shot—A ground stroke that is hit as a winner past the opponent, who is typically at the net.

pinpoint stance—The footwork pattern in the serve in which the back foot is slid next to the front foot during the backswing.

platform stance—The footwork pattern in the serve in which the feet are positioned about shoulder-width apart and stay in that position until ball contact.

power—The ability to do work in a certain unit of time, or explosive ability.

pressurized ball—A ball in a vacuum-sealed container.

pronation—Inward rotation of body parts, such as the rotation of the hand to a palm-down position or an inward turn of the ankle when the sole of the foot contacts the surface of the court.

punch volley—A shot that is hit before the ball bounces by using a very short stroke.

quickness—A powerful first step.

racket face—The string area of the racket.

racket face orientation—The angle of the racket face (or string plane) at the moment of ball contact.

racket head—The area of the racket frame containing the strings.

racket throat—The area of the racket frame between the head and handle.

ready position—The preparation stance as a player awaits the opponent's shot.

recovery step—The step following impact when the trail leg comes around with the follow-through.

response time—The time elapsed from the onset of a stimulus (e.g., the ball coming off the opponent's racket) to the completion of a movement.

semiwestern forehand grip—The grip in which the hand is placed halfway between the positions for the eastern and western forehand grips, which allows ease in hitting topspin without the constraints caused by using the western grip.

service hitch—The interruption of a smooth, continuously moving racket during the backswing of the serve.

service return—The stroke used to return an opponent's serve.

shoe last—The shape of the shoe's sole.

sidespin—Sideways rotation of the ball (like a top).

solid (heavy) ball—A high-velocity shot that is very penetrating to the opponent.

speed—The rate of change of a player's position. Specific to tennis, this refers to the highest velocity that a player can reach.

split-step—The preparation step as a player approaches the net, which squares up the body relative to the ball's possible flight pattern.

sport science—The application of scientific principles to sport, such as tennis.

static balance—Overall body control while standing still. *See also dynamic balance.*

stutter step—A short adjustment step taken to perfectly position the body for ball contact.

sweet spot—The central area on the tennis racket face, which, when impacted, results in minimal force to the hand.

toe box—The area of a shoe surrounding the toes.

topspin—Rotation of the top of the ball away from the player as the ball travels toward the opponent.

torque—The rotational force occurring around an axis (such as a joint in your body).

tracking—Following the ball with the eyes.

trajectory—The flight pattern of a ball.

underspin (or backspin)—Rotation of the top of the ball toward the player as the ball travels toward the opponent.

unit turn—The initial footwork and body rotation that should occur as a player prepares for a stroke.

unweighting—The reduction of force between the feet and the tennis court.

velocity—The rate of change of an object's position.

volley—A ball hit before it bounces.

western forehand grip—A grip that places the hand under the grip on the racket, which enables the player to hit ground strokes with heavy topspin but can create problems on low-bouncing balls.

References

An, B. (1979). A theoretical model of a physiologically natural grip for rackets in racket sports. In J. Groppel (Ed.), *Proceedings of a National Symposium on the Racket Sports* (pp. 141-158). University of Illinois at Urbana-Champaign, Division of Conferences and Institutes.

Baker, J., & Putnam, C. (1979). Tennis racket and ball responses during impact under clamped and freestanding conditions. *Research Quarterly, 50*, 164-170.

Blanksby, B., Elliott, B., & Ellis, R. (1979). Selecting the right racket: Performance characteristics of regular-sized and oversized tennis rackets. *Australian Journal of Health, Physical Education and Recreation, 86*, 21-25.

Braden, V., & Bruns, B. (1977). *Tennis for the future.* Boston: Little, Brown.

Brody, H. (1979). Physics of the tennis racket. *American Journal of Physics, 47*(6), 482-487.

Brody, H. (1981). Physics of the tennis racket II: The "sweet spot." *American Journal of Physics, 49*(9), 816-819.

Brody, H. (1987). *Tennis science for tennis players.* Philadelphia: University of Pennsylvania Press.

Broer, M., & Zernicke, R. (1979). *Efficiency of human movement.* Philadelphia: W.B. Saunders.

Bunn, M.R. (1960). *Scientific principles of coaching.* Englewood Cliffs, NJ: Prentice-Hall.

Cochan, A., & Stobbs, J. (1968). *Search for the perfect swing.* New York: J.B. Lippincott.

Daish, C.B. (1972). *Learn science through ball games.* London: English Universities Press.

Elliott, B.C. (1982). Tennis: The influence of grip tightness on reaction impulse and rebound velocity. *Medicine and Science in Sports and Exercise, (14)*5, 348-352.

Elliott, B., Blanksby, B., & Ellis, R. (1980). Vibrations and rebound velocity characteristics of conventional and oversized tennis rackets. *Research Quarterly for Exercise and Sport*, **51**, 608-615.

Elliott, B., & Kilderry, R. (1983). *The art and science of tennis.* Philadelphia: Saunders College Publishing.

Gonzales, P., & Hyams, J. (1974). *Winning tactics for weekend singles.* New York: Bantam Books.

Grabiner, M., Groppel, J., & Campbell, K. (1983). Resultant ball velocity as a function of grip firmness during off-center impacts in tennis. *Medicine and Science in Sports and Exercise*, **15**(6), 542-544.

Groppel, J. (1983a). Gut reactions. *World Tennis*, **31**(6), 28-30.

Groppel, J.L. (1983b). Teaching one- and two-handed backhand drives: Biomechanical considerations. *Journal of Physical Education and Recreation*, **54**(5), 23-26.

Groppel, J. (Ed.) (1988). *The USPTA sport science and sports medicine guide* (Vol. 1). Wesley Chapel, FL: United States Professional Tennis Association.

Groppel, J., Dillman, C., & Lardner, T. (1983). Derivation and validation of equations of motion to predict ball spin upon tennis impact. *Journal of Sport Sciences*, **1**, 111-120.

Groppel, J., Loehr, J., Melville, S., & Quinn, A. (1989). *Science of coaching tennis.*. Champaign, IL: Human Kinetics.

Groppel, J., Shin, I., Spotts, J., & Hill, B. (1987). Effects of different string tension patterns and racket motion on tennis racket–ball impact. *International Journal of Sport Biomechanics*, **3**, 142-158.

Groppel, J., Shin, I., Thomas, J., & Welk, G. (1987). The effects of string type and tension on impact in midsize and oversized tennis rackets. *International Journal of Sport Biomechanics*, **3**, 40-46.

Hatze, H. (1976). Forces and duration of impact, and grip tightness during the tennis stroke. *Medicine and Science in Sports*, **8**, 88-95.

Hensley, L.D. (1979). Analysis of stroking errors committed in championship tennis competition. In J. Groppel (Ed.), *Proceedings of a National Symposium on the Racket Sports* (pp. 225-236). University of Illinois at Urbana-Champaign, Division of Conferences and Institutes.

Hensley, L.D., & Norton, C. (1980). Success in tennis: Keep the ball in play. In J. Groppel (Ed.), *Proceedings of the International Symposium of the Effective Teaching of Racket Sports* (pp. 42-45). University of Illinois at Urbana-Champaign, Division of Conferences and Institutes.

Loehr, J. (1986). *Mental toughness training for sport.* Boston: Stephan Greene Press.

Loehr, J. (1990). *The mental game.* Boston: Stephan Greene Press.

Murphy, B., & Murphy, C. (1975). *Tennis for the player, teacher and coach.* Philadelphia: W.B. Saunders.

Orlick, T. (1980). *In pursuit of excellence.* Champaign, IL: Human Kinetics.

Plangenhoef, S. (1970). *Fundamentals of tennis*. Englewood Cliffs, NJ: Prentice-Hall.

Plangenhoef, S. (1971). *Patterns of human motion: A cinematographical analysis*. Englewood Cliffs, NJ: Prentice-Hall.

Plangenhoef, S. (1979). Tennis racket testing related to "tennis elbow." In J. Groppel (Ed.), *Proceedings of a National Symposium on the Racket Sports* (pp. 291-310). University of Illinois at Urbana-Champaign, Division of Conferences and Institutes.

Rand, K.T., Hyer, M.W., & Williams, M.H. (1979). A dynamic test for comparison of rebound characteristics of three brands of tennis balls. In J. Groppel (Ed.), *Proceedings of the National Symposium on the Racket Sports* (pp. 240-252). University of Illinois at Urbana-Champaign, Division of Conferences and Institutes.

Simpson, R.R. (1982). Foot and lower leg problems in racket sport athletes. In J. Groppel (Ed.), *Proceedings of a Fourth International Symposium on the Effective Teaching of Racket Sports* (pp. 33-35). University of Illinois Conferences and Institutes.

Tilmanis, G.A. (1975). *Advanced tennis for coaches, teachers and players*. Philadelphia: Lea and Febiger.

Van der Meer, D. (1982). *Dennis Van der Meer's complete book of tennis*. Norwalk, CT: Golf Digest/Tennis, Inc., New York Times.

Watanabe, T., Ikegami, Y., & Miyashita, M. (1979). Tennis: The effects of grip firmness on ball velocity after impact. *Medicine and Science in Sports*, **11**, 359-361.

Index

About the Author

Professional tennis coach, Jack Groppel, PhD, is the Executive Vice President of the Loehr-Groppel/Saddlebrook Sport Science Center in Wesley Chapel, Florida and the director of both tennis and sports and health development for Saddlebrook Resort. He was formerly the head of player development for Harry Hopman/Saddlebrook International Tennis. In 1987, Dr. Groppel became certified as a Master Professional of the United States Professional Tennis Association (USPTA) and received the organization's highest honor as its National Teaching Professional of the Year. He is the chairman of the National Sport Science Committee for the United States Tennis Association (USTA) and is on the National Steering Committee for the USTA Player Development Program.

Dr. Groppel is also a recognized authority in sport research. He served as a research associate to the United States Olympic Training Center and presented the keynote address at the 1984 Olympic Scientific Congress. His research has included performance analyses of over 12 sports, including work with such tennis greats as John McEnroe, Stan Smith, and Michael Chang.

In addition to being an adjunct associate professor in the Department of Exercise and Sport Sciences at the University of Florida, Dr. Groppel is the author of over 200 articles on fitness, nutrition, and stress. He has written or edited 10 books, including the first edition of this book, *Tennis for Advanced Players: And Those Who Would Like To Be*, and *Science of Coaching Tennis*, both published by Human Kinetics Publishers.